SNOWBALLS
taking chances

{ a biblical examination
of **Modern Christianity**

robert j. tedesco, jr.

TATE PUBLISHING & *Enterprises*

TATE PUBLISHING
& *Enterprises*

Snowballs Taking Chances
Copyright © 2006 by Robert J. Tedesco, Jr.

No part of this publication may be reproduced, stored in a retrieval system or transmitted in any way by any means, electronic, mechanical, photocopy, recording or otherwise without the prior permission of the author except as provided by USA copyright law.

All Scripture taken from the *Holy Bible, New International Version* ®, Copyright © 1973, 1978, 1984 by International Bible Society. Used by permission of Zondervan Publishing House. All rights reserved.

This book is designed to provide accurate and authoritative information with regard to the subject matter covered. This information is given with the understanding that neither the author nor Tate Publishing, LLC is engaged in rendering legal, professional advice. Since the details of your situation are fact dependent, you should additionally seek the services of a competent professional.

Book design copyright © 2006 by Tate Publishing, LLC. All rights reserved.
Cover design by Taylor Rauschkolb
Interior design by Lauren Weatherholt

Published in the United States of America

ISBN: 1-5988636-2-2
06.10.13

This book is dedicated to all the righteous men and women who have stood firm in their faith in the face of persecution, discouragement and temptation, providing inspiration to the rest of us. Thank you for fighting the good fight of faith and finishing the race.

ACKNOWLEDGMENTS

I would like to express the sincerest of gratitude and love to my wife, Alice, for supporting me throughout the process of writing this book by being a source of great spiritual wisdom and loving honesty. You are not only my partner in this life but my best friend as well, and your unwavering love for Christ has challenged me to be a better man.

Secondly, I would like to thank my children Joshua, Karine, Samuel and Christa for the tremendous joy and inspiration you bring to my life. Also, thank you for your patience with the countless times you had to hear "As soon as the book is done, we'll do this, that or the other." It will have been well worth the effort if it inspires you to live for Jesus.

Finally, and most importantly, I give thanks to the Father, Son and Holy Spirit for the gift of my salvation, as well as the calling to write this book and the strength to carry it out.

TABLE OF CONTENTS

Preface: Bridled Passion 9

Part I–Preparing for Battle
   1. State of the Union 15
   2. Mere "Progressive" Christianity 27
   3. Out of the Mud & Mire 39
   4. A Lamp, a Sword and a Stream 59
   5. Unshakable Faith 69
   6. The Counselor 83

First Intermission: If Only 99

Part II–Engaging the Battle
   7. The Devil in the Details 105
   8. Muddy Waters 115
   9. The Four Keys 131
  10. The Four Battlefields 141
  11. The Remnant 161

Second Intermission: Embracing Autumn 177

Part III–Leaving a Legacy
  12. The Legacy of Relationships 183
  13. The Legacy of Stewardship 205
  14. The Legacy of the Spirit 227
  15. A Time for Heroes 243

PREFACE
bridled passion

> *Psalm 78:3–4*
> *". . . What we have heard and known, what our fathers have told us - we will not hide them from (our) children; we will tell the next generation the praise worthy deeds of the Lord, his power and the wonders he has done."*

Passion is an intriguing piece in the make-up of the human condition. Unbridled passion has toppled the greatest of men, but guided passion has given rise to revolutions and revivals that have changed the face of history and religion. As I take a look around me, I often wonder if there is anything left, beyond animal instinct, that is capable of inspiring passion in the typical American, or the typical Christian for that matter.

As a nation founded on the Judeo-Christian ethic, the example of Christ should be our model for passionate heroism. But at some point in recent history, our nation has shifted from making heroes of men and women who lived passionate lives of integrity and righteous heroism to idolizing men and women of unbridled physical and sensual desires such as entertainers, sports stars and sex symbols. The future of this nation, and possibly humanity itself, rests on the ability of godly men and women to bridle their natural and physical passions, allowing them to be guided by a righteous desire to serve their Creator, even to their own peril.

This book was inspired by two passions of mine. First of all, God has blessed me with a beautiful wife and four wonderful children, all of whom will be shamelessly mentioned throughout this book. And if I could have one passion fulfilled before departing this life, it would be to see each one of these children give their lives into the loving and caring hands of Jesus Christ, my Savior. I would consider my life a waste if I did not do everything within my power to pass on the Christian faith to my children.

Second, I have a passion to see God's name glorified once again in this nation; to witness the name of Christ restored to a place of honor and prominence, instead of used as the profane expression of choice in our speech and entertainment. Our nation is presently engulfed by a dark and dreary, spiritual and moral fog; it is a fog of heaviness, confusion and depravity caused by an unwillingness to acknowledge the very God who created us. In the name of tolerance, we have abandoned the one and only Being who is able to burn off this fog and set us free. He is the one true living God, who sent His Son to break these chains that have bound us; but in many ways, we have rejected Him, both Christians and non-Christians alike.

As a result of this spiritual confusion, I believe that many people who would consider themselves active, church-going Christians have been lulled into a false sense of eternal security. I say this because very often the lives of those who attend church regularly don't look any different from those who don't, and if we are truly children of the Almighty God, our lives should reflect His glory in some way.

The Chance of a Snowball

One of the most sobering passages in Scripture is from Matthew 7:21–23,

> *"Not every one who says to me, 'Lord, Lord,' will enter the kingdom of heaven, but only he who does the will of my Father who is in heaven. Many will say to me on that day, 'Lord, Lord, did we not prophesy in your name, and in your name drive out demons and perform many miracles?' Then I will tell*

them plainly, 'I never knew you. Away from me, you evildoers.'"
- Jesus

According to the words of Jesus, *many* people will be deceived into thinking that their eternal security—their entrance into heaven—is a done deal. What is even more striking is that Jesus seems to be pointing out that even though some people might be actively involved in all sorts of ministry, they could still be turned away at the gates of heaven. This goes directly against the popular belief that only the worst, despicable sinners will be rejected by God.

It is my personal belief that the modern approach to Christianity has amplified this deception of the masses, and as a result, many people will one day hear those devastating words from Christ: "I never knew you." Our desire as Americans to avoid offending anyone has undoubtedly led to spiritual death for many. Scripture is filled with examples of societies that have taken similar paths, so the approach I would like to take with this book is to use Scripture to examine our culture, the Church, and our individual beliefs. One objective throughout will be to show how these three entities inevitably affect each other, and my ultimate purpose will be to challenge men and women to live passionate, victorious lives in Christ.

The Culture War

Whether we wish to acknowledge it or not, our American culture is at war with the Christian way of life, and in many cases, with Christ himself. Imagine moving to Israel and then demanding the removal of every mention or symbol of the Jewish faith. As ridiculous as this sounds, for some guilt-ridden reason, Americans feel obligated to purge public life—and soon private life—of the very God who has carried us to prominence.

Matthew 10:32–33 "Whoever acknowledges me before men, I will also acknowledge him before my Father in heaven. But

> *whoever disowns me before men, I will disown him before my Father in heaven." - Jesus*

The Scripture above applies not only to the individual but also to nations and churches. We can acknowledge Jesus by engaging the battle and resisting the temptation to sit idly by as the Name of Christ is dishonored in our society. If the Church is to be a factor in reclaiming this nation for Christ, we must first prepare for battle by honestly evaluating our culture and our own faith in light of Holy Scripture (Part I of this book). Once we do this, we are then able to engage this cultural battle (Part II). The "battle" I will mention throughout the book will not primarily refer to the one we fight outwardly against institutions and corporations who refuse to acknowledge Christ; after all, if we need to rely on government or corporate America to keep Christianity alive, it is time to check the oil in the lamp. No, the battle I will focus on will be the inward battle for the soul and for righteousness and holiness. If we win *this* battle, it will lend spiritual legitimacy and integrity to the outward battles God calls us to fight. Finally, we must not only fight the good fight, but we should simultaneously affect positive change on our society by using all of our resources and talents for the glory of God; this is our legacy (Part III).

It is my prayer that this book moves the reader forward in all of these areas, and that the words I use will be inspired by the Holy Spirit, challenging Christians to live in a manner worthy of the calling.

> *1 Corinthians 1:17 ". . . for Christ did not send me to baptize, but to preach the Gospel—not with words of human wisdom, lest the cross be emptied of its power."*

PART 1
preparing for battle

CHAPTER 1
state of the union

    Several years ago, I heard a discussion on the radio about passion and impeachment. Our nation's legislators were engaged in a heated debate on morality, honesty, and the legal ramifications of the subsequent lack thereof, and the debate was just about as coherent as the beginning of this sentence. At the time I tuned into the discussion, I heard someone speaking about how our nation is "on the edge of an abyss," and if we take that fatal step, it would plunge the nation into ruin. Now, because I hadn't heard the beginning of the discussion, I assumed the speaker was making reference to the condition of morality in our nation and that he was expressing his concern that our nation was on the edge of a moral free-fall that would surely be the demise of our once-great nation.

    So, you can imagine my surprise when it occurred to me that he was speaking about the dangers of holding our high officials to standards that no one could live up to. The abyss he was referring to was the shortage of qualified applicants for government offices that we would experience once we, as a nation, start holding them accountable for the actions in their "private lives." He contended that it was unrealistic to hope for men and women of integrity as elected officials, and that we would do our nation a disservice by having these lofty standards. The common sentiment around the nation was that moral character was not an issue when choosing a president. At the time, I remember thinking, *At this rate of moral decline, it won't be long before we'll be able to compare notes with those who witnessed the fall of the Roman Empire.*

Judicial Tyranny

Now fast-forward several years to the time of the writing of this book, and we get a clear glimpse of why moral character might be at least slightly important when choosing a leader. As I write, there are a few court cases in the news being presided over by judicial appointees that highlight the moral hypocrisy we are experiencing in our nation. The most publicized is the case involving Terri Schiavo, who, as I see it, was allowed to starve to death in a hospice bed because her loving husband suddenly remembered (possibly while at his girlfriend's house) that she wouldn't want to live this way. The whole debate over her life was framed with the question, "Would *you* want to live this way?"

Each night as I watch the evening news, I am continually reminded that I would not want to live like ninety percent of the world's population, but I still don't think we should starve them as a means of putting them out of their misery. Nevertheless, some Supreme Court justices now consider themselves masters of the universe who will decide *for us* the value of life and who should live or die.

While Terri was being starved to death and gasping for just a drop of water, there was another court case in Colorado where a judge overturned the sentence of a convicted murderer and rapist because the jury had the audacity to consult Scripture while deciding the fate of the murderer. The judge was concerned that the words of God—the Author of all life—could have influenced the jury's decision.

And finally, again while Terri was starving, a local story topped the news of all the Pittsburgh new stations, which really amplified how confused our society has become. A hysterical woman appeared on camera, visibly disturbed with tears streaming down her cheeks, pleading for help from the Pittsburgh community. You see, she worked for an animal shelter, which had a "*No Kill*" policy, and they had reached their capacity for saving these tortured animals. She tearfully recounted the story of one emaciated dog, which had been neglected—possibly starved—by its owner. Now I certainly believe we should protect all of God's creation; we adopted our dog, Shadow, from an animal shelter. But I couldn't help thinking to myself, *If Terri's loving husband had dropped her off at the animal shelter, she would have gotten far better treatment and press coverage, and for seventy bucks and no court battle, her parents could have adopted her and taken care of her.*

As I contemplated these three stories, it occurred to me—I was wrong. Our nation isn't in a moral free-fall, or on a slippery slope, or any other catchy phrase you want to use. We've hit bottom.

> *Ecclesiastes 3:16–17 And I saw something else under the sun:* ***In the place of judgment****—wickedness was there,* ***in the place of justice****—wickedness was there. I thought in my heart, "God will bring to judgment both the righteous and the wicked, for there will be a time for every activity, a time for every deed." (emphasis added)*

Sometimes it is astounding how accurate and relevant Scripture is when describing the plight of humanity, but the Bible would be a depressing book if it did not provide answers to these problems. There is a Scripture passage I believe accurately paints a portrait of where we find ourselves as a nation, but I will preface it by saying that this book will be more about the "solution" rather than the "problem."

> *2 Timothy 3:1–5 "But mark this: there will be terrible times in the last days. People will be lovers of themselves, lovers of money, proud, abusive, disobedient to parents, ungrateful, unholy, without love, unforgiving, slanderous, without self-control, brutal, not lovers of the good, treacherous, rash, conceited,* ***lovers of pleasure*** *rather than lovers of God—****having a form of godliness but denying its power****. Have nothing to do with them . . ." (emphasis added)*

I would be a fool to try to predict the end-times. But you have to admit; we do bear striking resemblance to the society described above.

State of Confusion

What we are witnessing in our country is a hysterical chaos that can only be caused by a spiritual confusion and blindness. Spiritual blindness occurs when the people of a nation decide to boldly declare their self-reliance by rejecting God and his existence, and with their newfound wisdom and intellectual prowess they spit in the face of God as they embark on a quest to create their own truth and morality. Thus moral relativism is born. In history, this has always happened after a nation reaches prosperity and decides it no longer needs God. It is the Titanic philosophy that says, "Not even God could sink this ship." If we were to try to address the individual ills of our country, it would be much like "rearranging the chairs on the deck of the Titanic." Unless we change our course, we'll be calling out to God from the icy waters.

The Basis for Law and Order

For a nation to govern itself it needs a system of laws. To set up laws, legislators need a standard by which to decide right from wrong. So it only makes sense that when you attempt to purge the one true God from society, you lose that immovable, unchanging standard by which to judge. Truth and morality become relative to each person's beliefs, and all decency and order are sacrificed. This is the chaos we are beginning to experience as we find ourselves debating the importance of character, virtue, truth, and ultimately, the meaning of the word "is."

In the book of Jeremiah, we are given an example of this type of chaos. At that time, the culture of Israel had degenerated so much that each man just followed his physical passions, regardless of where they led him or what the divine consequences would be. With that in mind, let's read what God had to say through the prophet Jeremiah about the prospect of judgment they were about to face.

Jeremiah 5:7–9 "I supplied all their needs, yet they committed adultery and thronged to the houses of prostitutes. They are well-fed, lusty stallions, each neighing for another man's wife. Should I not avenge myself on a nation such as this?"

Every night on television you'll find countless programs making light of the very issues that have caused the destruction of nations. Is it any wonder that our teens seem so confused on issues of morality? For example, I recently took my family to an amusement park, and I thought I had accidentally scheduled our trip on "Pajama Day at the Park," because many of the teen girls (and pre-teens) were wearing camisoles. As it turned out, the eveningwear just happened to be the latest trend in women's fashion, but the downward trend away from simple modesty is just symptomatic of the much more significant problems of spiritual and moral decay.

Spiritual Blindness

So as we take a look around us, we ask, "How could there be so much blindness to the truth? How depraved can a society become before they cease to exist?" Jesus brings some clarity to the first question when He says, "Blessed are the pure in heart, for they will see God." (Mt. 5:8)

To "see" God spiritually is to know His ways, and "the truth will set you free." (Jn. 8:32) Conversely, we could say, "Cursed are the impure in heart, for they shall not see God."

As I see it, the problem of spiritual blindness has many components, but two of the most significant contributors are the rejection of the Creator by our society and the impurity of those who call themselves by His Name.

Zephaniah 1:17 "I will bring distress on the people and they will walk like blind men, because they have sinned against the Lord."

Later in the book, I'll examine the effects of sin and impurity on the Church and on the nation, but for now I'd like to focus on how this state of blindness has affected the expression of faith in America. This is quite effectively illustrated by an article in *Life* magazine from December, 1998. It was written by Frank McCourt and was entitled, "When you think of God, what do you see?" It is indicative of the spiritual confusion in our society, so I'd like to quote some portions of the article.

The first is about the "richness" of life we experience by having so many gods in our nation:

> *"Americans, answerable only to their god, can choose (which god to follow). The sweet irony is that the United States has become a most god-fearing nation. By allowing the garden to grow as it will, we enjoy a multifarious bounty—one nation under gods… George Washington said in his farewell address that 'religion and morality are indispensable supports' of the American idea. Those supports, ever strong, grow stronger."*

I'm not sure I would classify America as "god-fearing nation," since fear of God, by definition, should produce reverence followed by obedience. In America, I'm not sure I see signs of either. "Those supports, ever strong, grow stronger" he says. Really? Fear of God, morality, and religion continue to decline in our country, but the point he goes on to make is that the number of people (96%) that believe in *a* god (of their choice) is up drastically. He continues:

> *"I don't confine myself to the faith of my fathers anymore. All the religions are spread before me, a great spiritual smorgasbord, and I'll help myself, thank you."*

The following percentages represent the findings upon which Mr. McCourt bases his conclusions:

> *96% of Americans believe in (a) god.*
> *33% believe that the Bible is the Word of God.*
> *80% believe in an after-life.*

72% believe in Heaven.
56% believe in Hell.
79% pray to god and feel he has helped them make decisions.

This all-you-can-stomach spiritual buffet mentality is the height of spiritual confusion, not enlightenment. It is like going to a "god fair" at the Expo Mart and collecting pamphlets on all the different gods, and then carrying them around as proof that you belong to each of them. But it is not uncommon to hear even Christians say that we are all searching for God in our own way, and all that really matters is that each one of us is serving a higher power of some sort. In order to persist in this type of belief, we have to completely ignore the first two Commandments:

Exodus 20:3,4,5a
"You shall have no other gods before me."
"You shall not make for yourself an idol in the form of anything in Heaven above or on the earth beneath or in the waters below. You shall not bow down to worship them; for I the Lord Your God, am a jealous God . . ."

What I find disturbing is, the further we travel down this multicultural-all-gods-are-equal road, the more we begin to resemble the Athenian society of the first century described in the book of Acts. The men of Athens considered themselves enlightened, coffee-shop intellectuals who were quite proud of the vast collection of gods they had amassed. As you read this next Scripture passage, I believe you will find the Athenian culture to be eerily similar to the one praised by Frank McCourt earlier in this chapter. To set it up, Paul had been preaching the good news about Christ, and the Athenians found themselves intrigued with the possibility of adding a new god to their list; his teaching was the first they had heard about Jesus.

Acts 17:19b-23 "'May we know what this new teaching is that you are presenting? You are bringing some strange ideas to our ears, and we want to know what they mean.' (All the Athenians and the foreigners who lived there spent their time doing nothing but talking about and listening to the latest ideas.)"

"Paul then stood up in the meeting of the Areopagus and said: 'Men of Athens! I see that in every way you are very religious. For as I walked around and looked carefully at your objects of worship, I even found an altar with this inscription: TO AN UNKNOWN GOD. Now what you worship as something unknown I am going to proclaim to you.'"

In this passage, Paul is either being sarcastic by calling them "religious," or he is attempting to win their graces by commenting on their open-mindedness, but I assure you, he was not paying them a compliment. And if their culture was in need of a missionary like Paul, how much more is ours? But even Christians are beginning to accept the premise that expressing their faith is somehow intolerant, and as a result, the sense of urgency for missions is being diminished.

Later in the passage, Paul goes on to preach to them about the God of all creation, and then warns them that God will no longer tolerate the crafting of false gods and idols, since the resurrection of Christ should serve as proof that He is the One true God. Paul finishes by saying,

Acts 17:30–31 "In the past God overlooked such ignorance, but now he commands all people everywhere to repent. For he has set a day when he will judge the world with justice by the man he has appointed. He has given proof of this to all men by raising him from the dead."

With a proclamation like that, Paul makes himself a prime candidate for a sensitivity training seminar, because he is calling the Athenians to repent of their polytheistic religious practices, or the worship of many gods. To a society of Greeks who considered themselves intellectuals, I believe he lost the crowd when he mentioned the word "ignorance." Paul's words were met with a collective, yet enlightened, Athenian yawn.

> *Acts 17:32–34 "When they heard about the resurrection of the dead, some of them sneered, but others said, 'We want to hear you again on this subject.' At that, Paul left the Council. A few men became followers of Paul and believed."*

As you can see, the Athenians did not fall to their knees in repentance and tears; only a "few men" had a change of heart. Amazingly, Paul's words are just as relevant today as they were in the first century, and we will need to decide how to respond to them. The Greeks had the excuse of not having heard the Scriptures or the prophets, which explains why "in the past God overlooked such ignorance." But we as a nation have seen the bounty of God's blessing and are fully aware of Jesus' death and resurrection, so we do not have the option of pleading "ignorance."

Reuniting Church and State

So where does all this leave us as a nation? The founders of this country established it as "one nation, under God," not *gods*, and we must find a way to return to that foundational principle. Somehow, the policy of the separation of Church and State has devolved into an excuse not to require moral integrity from our elected officials, because after all, "that would be judging, and by whose god will we ultimately derive our standard?" This type of reasoning would be laughable if it weren't so prevalent, but you can see the inevitable result of sacrificing our religious convictions on the altar of sensitivity.

So as Christians, we must remove our tails from between our legs and begin defending our beliefs, even if it means showing our teeth now and then. One of the best ways of doing this—and effectively reuniting Church and State—is by holding our leaders to only the highest of Judeo-Christian standards and letting God deal with the shortage of applicants for office. The issues of morality and ethics we are currently facing in America trump any of the pocketbook or political issues on the table, and besides, it is more likely that God will prosper a nation that places Him first.

> *Psalm 33:12 "Blessed is the nation whose God is the Lord, the people he chose for his inheritance."*

On the other hand, for those who believe that the separation of Church and State means telling the Creator of the universe to stay out of our business when it comes to the election of our politicians, Scripture quite accurately predicts the inevitable course of such a nation.

> *Hosea 8:14, 9:15, 10:3–4 "They set up kings without my consent; they choose princes without my approval . . . Because of their sinful deeds, I will drive them out of my house. I will no longer love them; all their leaders are rebellious . . . Then they will say: 'We have no king because we did not revere the Lord. But even if we had a king, what could he do for us? They make many promises, take false oaths and make agreements; therefore lawsuits spring up like poisonous weeds in a plowed field.'"*

As I read about the ongoing sagas of all of our indicted and incarcerated officials, I can't help but be amazed by the relevancy and clarity of Scripture. But why should I be surprised? It is the Word of God—His handbook to the meaning of life, the origin of the universe, eternal life, social ills and anything else we choose to explore. From that perspective, it is quite entertaining to listen to "thinkers" on radio and television talk shows explore their minds for the answers to human behavior and morality, when the answers are right there in the hotel bed-stand (for now). The best parallel I can think of is the philosophy "When all else fails, read the directions." It sounds trite, but nonetheless, it is true.

A few years back, my son Joshua came to me one evening after having put together a toy he received earlier that day, and he was bursting with pride because he had finished it without any assistance. So I put down the book I was reading entitled, *Americans and Government: Take My Money, Take My Freedom, Even Take the Minds of My Children, but Please Don't Take My Plasma TV* (you haven't heard of it because I haven't written it yet), and I asked him, "How in the heck did you do that all by yourself?"

He replied, "I followed the directions." and it became obvious to me that my wife was beginning to have a bad influence on him.

Sometimes the answer is that obvious; follow the instructions sent by the manufacturer. My son could have tried to use the instructions from his sister Karine's Easy-Bake Oven to help him build his toy, but he would have had considerably less success.

By the end of this book, I hope to dispel the notion that the Bible is outdated or irrelevant, thereby instilling a desire to know the *Author* of Scripture. For this reason, you will find many Scripture passages scattered throughout the book, and I will quote the passage rather than just give reference to it. I'll do this because if you are anything like the typical American, myself included, you are short on time and patience and would rather not take the time to look up the reference while you are reading.

Marshmallow Peep Theology

Ultimately, "The State of the Union" has more to do with the spiritual state of its individuals than it does with its elected officials. Earlier, I suggested we un-tuck our tails and defend our Christian faith; but in order to do that, each one of us needs to first examine what we believe in light of the words of Scripture, and very often, this is where it gets murky.

Recently, I was asked to give a sharing to a group of teens about worship, and I decided to speak about the "Who and why" of worship, instead of the "how." It was during lent, and to my utter joy, lent is the time of year when the first sightings of marshmallow Peeps on grocery store shelves begin to occur. Anyway, I spoke to the teens about how the expression of our faith in America is beginning to resemble a marshmallow Peep—soft, squishy, covered in sugary sweetness, more palatable when it is stale, and of no spiritual-nutritional value whatsoever. Just as an example, when we say, "Christianity is one of the many ways to find God," it sounds real nice and sweet, but it renders the crucifixion of Christ useless. Jesus becomes an "also-ran," and then our faith is meaningless.

This gradual shift in Christian theology over the years has gone largely unnoticed to the average churchgoer, and it will take a concerted, Biblically based effort to shift it back. So clinging to the words of Scripture, we move forward.

Zec. 14:9 The Lord will be King over the whole earth. On that day there will be one Lord, and his name the only name.

CHAPTER 2
mere "progressive" christianity

The Impostor

The greatest plague facing our nation today is not crime, or racism, or adultery, or divorce, or abortion, or promiscuous teens. These are all painful and devastating symptoms, which grieve the heart of Christ, but they are caused by a much more deeply rooted disease—a disease I'll call "Progressive Christianity." I say this because *true* Christianity, when lived out according to Biblical standards, holds the remedy and the cure to all these social ills. But God's people must first turn to Him in humility:

> *2 Chronicles 7:14 " . . . if my people, who are called by my name, will humble themselves and pray and seek my face and turn from their wicked ways, then I will hear from heaven and will forgive their sin and will heal their land."*

In studying the history of Judaism or Christianity, our God has always held the people who call themselves by His name to a higher standard—*His*. If we were to adhere to His standard, our lives would transform the world around us. But as we glance around at the pew or the chair next to us, and we see the hurt and the pain and the broken families, we force a smile and say, "God bless you" or "Peace be with you."

> *Jeremiah 8:11 "They dress the wound of my people as though it were not serious. 'Peace, peace,' they say, when there is no peace."*

What we are witnessing in America—not to mention around the entire globe—is the wasting away of our very beings. The destruction of the traditional family and the devaluing of human life are sure signs of the decay that has taken hold, and we need to look no further than ourselves, the Church, as we search for the answer.

Recognizing Progressive Christianity

I'd like to focus on the word "progressive" because of the way it is being used in our culture, specifically within the Church. I've recently heard some well-intentioned (and some not-so-well-intentioned) members of various Christian denominations call for the leadership of their denominations to be more progressive. Usually what "progressive" means is that Church leadership should stop being so mean-spirited and rigid on issues of morality. Now, as enlightened and forward-thinking as that may sound, a close examination of that school of thought reveals at least one serious intellectual flaw. When someone chooses—or rejects—a religion, that person, by virtue of his choice, is either acknowledging or denying the existence of a heavenly being or higher power whose standards are the basis for that particular religion. In the case of Christianity, the role of church leadership (in regard to doctrine) is to simply relate the doctrines of Christ to the congregation, not to mold the doctrines into something more progressive. The doctrines of Scripture are alive through Christ, but the Bible is not meant to be a living, breathing document to be changed at the whim of the majority.

The only reason I bother pointing out this inconsistency in progressive theology (which in itself is an oxymoron), is because I believe there are some honest Christians who wholeheartedly support these "new and improved" ideas without ever having considered how contrary to Scripture they really are. Unfortunately, the reality probably is that most of the people screaming for the Church to be more progressive are not actively involved in an honest search to know their Savior.

It is more likely that they view the Church as one more cultural institution needing to be purged of its intolerant ways.

The Post-Christian Era

Most Americans, when asked, would probably classify themselves as Christians, yet we live in a post-Christian era. How is this possible? Because the definition of "Christian" has been watered down so significantly that it no longer means anything more than you affiliate yourself with a particular group of people or with certain holiday rituals.

In his book "Mere Christianity," C.S. Lewis explains this cheapening of the word *Christian* by comparing it to the word *gentleman*.

> *"The word gentleman originally meant something recognizable; one who had a coat of arms and some landed property. When you called someone 'a gentleman' you were not paying him a compliment, but merely stating a fact. If you said he was not 'a gentleman' you were not insulting him, but giving information. There was no contradiction in saying that John was a liar and a gentleman; any more than there now is in saying that James is a fool and an M.A."*

He goes on to explain how the word *gentleman* eventually became a term of praise, describing how a man of standing should act, as opposed to a term relating facts about the individual. His point was (at the time) the word Christian was quickly becoming a term of praise, describing how a person should act, as opposed to describing someone who "accepts the common doctrines of Christianity." Little did he know, the word *Christian* would eventually become a derogatory term, meaning . . .

> *"One who stubbornly and intolerantly adheres to the oppressive doctrines of his faith, as he sits on his front porch cleaning his rifle. Also, a Christian is one who regularly violates our constitutional right to 'Freedom from religion,' and one who wishes to spoil all the fun we are inherently entitled to as Americans, as*

it is clearly written in the Bill of Rights, somewhere." (Revised definition mine)

Luckily for us, the modern culture says that it is okay to be Christian, at least for the present, as long as you don't believe anything in particular, and as long as you don't mention anything in public that resembles an absolute or moral position. "And for goodness sake, get those mean Commandments off the courthouse walls."

Sooner or later, our society will become so hostile toward Christianity that there will no longer be such a thing as a "progressive Christian," because each of us will be forced to take a position. Christians around the world are being martyred daily, yet we barely put up a struggle as the progressives convert "freedom of religion" to "freedom *from* religion." At what point will we stand up and say, "No more!"? Can somebody out there tell me where all the cowboys have gone? Where is that pioneering spirit of the founding fathers that says, "We will fight to the death!"?

I believe I will start answering my own questions in the next section as I relate a few more modern-day news stories. And you'll see that passion isn't necessarily dead; its priorities have just shifted a little.

The Abolition of Manhood

A couple of days before writing this, on my local news channel there was a story about Carnegie Mellon University in Pittsburgh. Apparently one of the student activities sponsored by the university was the showing of a pornographic film, and more than 3000 students showed up to watch it. The news footage showed hundreds of students, mostly guys, packed into a hallway, attempting to get into the auditorium. Not surprisingly, the faculty made no apologies for the film or for the fact that student activity fees paid for it. No doubt, if the movie had been "The Passion of the Christ," it would have inspired a student-led hunger strike, with distraught protestors chained to an early 70s model VW van.

In another story about misguided passion, a few days before the incident above, my TV was graced with the coverage of "Black Friday," or the official opening day of the "Annual Gift-buying for Deity-neutral Holidays Extravaganza." The evening news coverage showed grown men—who had waited in the cold for hours, much like Washington during the American Revolution—jockeying for position to get their hands on the latest gaming console, and in some cases, following people home and robbing them, if necessary.

This story was followed by footage of men and women trampling each other at retail stores around the country, all for the pathetic purpose of getting their hands on deals that would be readily available for weeks afterward. Now, to their credit, some of the men proved that chivalry was not entirely dead by pushing the women who were lying on the floor off to the side, instead of stepping right on them; Merry Christmas. Oops. I should have said "Happy Holidays."

As a side note, this particular year many retailers continued their systematic removal of any mention of the name of Christ during the *Christ*mas holiday—undoubtedly an honest and sincere effort to, on one hand, ensure everyone's season would be bright, and on the other, still get to keep the holiday cash.

> *Isaiah 60:12 For the nation or kingdom that will not serve you will perish; it will be utterly ruined.*

We need to keep this verse in mind as we continue the removal of the name of Christ from our culture.

Returning to the topic of misguided passion, I would like to recount a final example of how the abolition of manhood is affecting the modern Church. During the same week as the previous two news stories, there was a controversy brewing within the Roman Catholic Church. Pope Benedict XVI had issued a document restricting the activities of homosexual men entering the priesthood, and a firestorm of criticism was ignited throughout the country. The Pope was taken to task, rather passionately, for suggesting that those who have struggled with the homosexual lifestyle must have overcome their tendencies for a period of three years before joining the seminary.

In an article by Joan Garry for the USA Today (Nov. 30, 2005), she states that the Church is "making a choice that doesn't feel very Christian." In other words, we are to assume that a "Christian" choice is one that doesn't hurt anyone's feelings, regardless whether or not it is consistent with scripture. So let me ask this: If I wanted to be a referee for the NFL, but I didn't agree with all the pushing and shoving and tackling, should their personnel department overlook this small detail during the interviewing process?

Joan Garry inadvertently underscores the need for a wakeup call within the Christian Church as she quotes her own mother. "We all knew a lot of priests we figured were gay," my mom told me. "If they did a good job, so what?"

What does that *mean*? "If they did a good *job* . . ."? Are we not talking about the house of God? Are we not talking about imparting the Holy Scriptures to God's people? Are we not talking about counseling young people on sexuality and morality? How can a man who disagrees with the fundamental beliefs of the Church genuinely uphold Christ's teachings? If the leaders of the Church are not in a position to uphold a moral standard, who is?

These "progressive" beliefs have become deeply rooted in just about all Christian denominations, and we can no longer sit idly by while the Church—and consequently, the nation—deteriorates toward Godlessness. Make no mistake about it; the inevitable result of progressive Christianity is nonexistent Christianity.

So what we glean from the stories above is first, we have a generation of men morphing into something very closely resembling the typical male portrayed by the vast majority of sitcoms and beer commercials. He is a thirty-something, perpetual adolescent with no core moral or ethical standards, and he is expected by society to suppress any natural, "chauvinistic" tendencies that cause him to want to protect and provide. Second, we see a Church that is hamstrung by a society that repeatedly tells the Church to stay out of its moral business. These two trends may not seem linked at first, but both have their roots in progressive thought, and both inevitably feed off each other. A weakened Church produces complacent and timid men, and as a result, those men allow the Church to continue to deteriorate.

Lessons Not Learned

For one brief moment in recent American history, men were allowed to be men, and God was allowed to be God. When our nation was attacked on September 11, 2001, there emerged two images on our TV screens that were diametrically opposed to everything we have been taught by our university professors and the media over the past forty years. The first was the image of the fireman rushing into the burning building, without any regard for his own life, to save the lives of others. The second was the image of America, as a whole, turning to God in prayer and fasting and attending church in record numbers. It was the unification of Church and State at its best, and none of the usual media suspects were running stories about keeping God out of public life. Regarding the former image, there were even polls showing that women preferred the strong, fireman/policeman type over the sensitive, lover-not-a-fighter type—and no one complained.

So out of the tragic rubble emerged a vivid, albeit short-lived, moment of moral and theological clarity. But, as those horrific pictures fade from our minds, so does the clarity. For years we had been told that the emperor of the Land of Progressive Theology and Gender Neutrality was dressed in a magnificent robe, and on 9/11, America was undoubtedly shocked by his/her nakedness. But it takes a healthy Church to sustain any of the lessons learned from historic events such as these, and the progressive seamstresses have been hard at work recreating the imaginary robe.

The Great Suggestion?

My objective for comparing the spiritual health of men to the spiritual condition of the Church is not to begin a long dissertation on the roles of men and women in society, but to show how society influences the individual, and in turn, how this affects the Church. And I believe that until the Church becomes spiritually healthy, our nation's slide toward secularism, hedonism and narcissism will continue. I've heard it said, "The church is not a museum for saints, but a hospital for sinners," which is very true, indeed. The problem is, because of the short-staffed condition of the church, people are not being cared for properly and in many cases, have not even been truly introduced to the Great Physician.

Matthew 9:36–38 When he saw the crowds, he had compassion on them, because they were harassed and helpless, like sheep without a shepherd. Then he said to his disciples, "The harvest is plentiful, but the workers are few. Ask the Lord of the harvest, therefore, to send out workers into his harvest field."

In addition to being short-handed, the wavering convictions and beliefs of the culture cause pastors great reluctance when addressing the truly relevent topics of the day, fearing they will labeled as being too "political." Instead, it is more likely we will hear from the pulpit some variation of the theme "God is love, and love is God, and as long as we all love each other, love will find a way;" it's safe, inoffensive, and unlikely to negatively affect the offering plate.

Scripture has a whole lot to say about contemporary issues such as the value of life, morality, truth, marriage, and sexuality, but I believe pastors sometimes feel forced to make self-preserving decisions when choosing which topics to address. This approach might temporarily save the building itself, but it will plunge the whole church into ruin. Jesus tells us in *The Great Commission* to " . . . go and make disciples of all the nations" (Mt. 28:19), not "Go make converts, and then keep them happy." When the primary objective of discipleship is sacrificed in favor of institutional survival, we end up with a hollow shell of religion that Christ calls "lukewarm" in Revelation 3:15–17:

"I know your deeds, that you are neither cold nor hot. I wish you were either one or the other! So, because you are lukewarm—neither hot nor cold—I am about to spit you out of my mouth. You say, 'I am rich; I have acquired wealth and do not need a thing.' But you do not realize that you are wretched, pitiful, poor, blind and naked."

The Hospice Mentality

As a result of this lukewarm condition, the church is beginning to resemble a hospice instead of a hospital; in other words, it is a place where terminally ill patients go to die. Very often, as members of the congregation, we act as though it is the Church's job to keep us comfortable until we pass away—a sort of death with dignity. "Just give us enough God in a spiritual eye dropper to relieve our dried up conscience, but not enough to actually promote healing." Our souls cry out for salvation and for spiritual refreshment, but the enemy of our souls uses our flesh to say, "No water of the Spirit is to be given to that soul under any circumstances! And no scriptures of rehabilitation—I own this soul and by my choice, it is destined for death!"

Psalm 63:1–3, 8 O God, you are my God, earnestly I seek you; my soul thirsts for you, my body longs for you, in a dry and weary land where there is no water. I have seen you in the sanctuary and beheld your power and your glory. Because your love is better than life, my lips will glorify you . . . My soul clings to you; your right hand upholds me.

Equipping for Battle

I've spent the last two chapters venting about the condition of our nation and the Church, so it might seem like this is the most natural place to start offering solutions. But since this is a spiritual battle we are facing, we should first spend some time solidifying the core beliefs of our faith before attempting to go into battle. These fundamentals should be common to all Christian denominations, so I'll apologize ahead of time for leaving out any denominational essentials that many would consider foundational to the practice of their faith.

It is almost impossible to talk about equipping Christians for battle without mentioning the popular Scripture passage from Ephesians relating to "The Armor of God." Actually, my prideful tendency is to want to avoid it altogether just because it is used so often, but I guess its frequent use speaks volumes about the timeless truths within it.

> **Ephesians 6:10–18** *The Armor of God*
> *"Finally, be strong in the Lord and in his mighty power. Put on the full armor of God so that you can take your stand against the devil's schemes.* ***For our struggle is not against flesh and blood,*** *but against the rulers, against the authorities, against the powers of this dark world and against the spiritual forces of evil in the heavenly realms.* ***Therefore put on the full armor of God,*** *so that when the day of evil comes, you may be able to stand your ground, and after you have done everything, to stand. Stand firm then, with the* ***belt of truth*** *buckled around your waist, with the* ***breastplate of righteousness*** *in place, and with your feet fitted with the readiness that comes from the* ***gospel of peace****. In addition to all this, take up the* ***shield of faith****, with which you can extinguish the flaming arrows of the evil one. Take the* ***helmet of salvation*** *and the* ***sword of the Spirit,*** *which is the word of God.* ***And pray in the Spirit*** *on all occasions with all kinds of prayers and requests. With this in mind, be alert and always keep on praying for all the saints." (emphasis added)*

I won't necessarily be methodically explaining each piece of armor in the traditional sense, but many of the next several chapters will include some key elements of this incredible Scripture passage. Below the title of each chapter, I'll mention the pieces of armor, if any, that are dealt with in some way within that chapter.

Since part of the premise for this book is the possibility that some people will be deceived into thinking they will spend eternity in heaven, it would only make sense for the next chapter to address the issue of salvation before attempting to move forward.

CHAPTER 3
out of the mud & mire

The Breastplate of Righteousness & the Helmet of Salvation

Have You Received Your Invitation?

I haven't personally done this, but I am sure many people have received a wedding invitation in the mail and secretly thought to themselves, "The meal at the reception better be at least as expensive as the gift I'm bringing. I'd better leave the card unsealed in case they serve the usual dried-up rigatoni and chicken-jerky."

Now, what if you received an invitation to a wedding that said, "An exquisite meal will be served following the ceremony, on the condition that you do not bring any gifts or cards. Additionally, those guests who arrive in formal attire will receive a $10,000 gift card to a spa or the home improvement store of your choice." For most of us, our response would be something like, "Are you kidding me? For *that* I would walk through a 'Mothers Against Torturous Child Programming (MATCaP)' meeting with a sign on my back that reads, 'Barney is my friend.'"

The Wedding Banquet

In the book of Matthew, Jesus uses *The Parable of the Wedding Banquet* as an analogy for the kingdom of heaven. In this parable, a king sends out invitations for his son's wedding banquet, only to have the recipients refuse to come. In response, he dispatches his servants to find out the reason for their refusal to attend.

Matthew 22:5–7 "But they (those invited) paid no attention and went off—one to his field, another to his business. The rest seized his servants, mistreated them and killed them. The king was enraged. He sent his army and destroyed those murderers and burned their city."

In hindsight, they would have probably been better off going to the wedding. The king then proceeded to invite anyone and everyone who would listen, regardless of their position in society, to come to his son's wedding banquet, and they were able to fill the wedding hall. Now the next part of the parable seems rather harsh, considering these people weren't supposed to be there in the first place.

Matthew 22:11–14 "But when the king came in to see the guests, he noticed a man there who was not wearing wedding clothes. 'Friend,' he asked, 'how did you get in here without wedding clothes?' The man was speechless.
"Then the king told the attendants, 'Tie him hand and foot, and throw him outside, into the darkness, where there will be weeping and gnashing of teeth.'
"For many are invited, but few are chosen."

This is one of those confusing parables that would be easier to discard than to try to get it to make sense with what we know about the character of the Father. The problem is, it deals with the issue of salvation, and Christ would not have used this parable unless he intended for it to carry great significance. Also, it addresses one of the most common misconceptions about salvation within the modern Church, so I would like to take some time to examine it more closely.

The Original Guest List

As Christ was teaching, He was aware of the watchful eyes of the chief priests and Pharisees and knew they were searching for a way to arrest Him. In the parable, the original guest list was meant to represent the Israelites, who were to be the first recipients of the invitation *out of the mud & mire*

to receive the gift of salvation offered through Christ—to attend the eternal banquet for the Son. For hundreds of years, the prophets had foretold the coming of the Savior, but once He was among them, He was rejected, in fulfillment of Psalm 118:22–23.

> "The stone the builders rejected has become the capstone; the Lord has done this, and it is marvelous in our eyes."

You see, the *anticipation* of the Messiah had become such a deeply rooted Jewish tradition that when He finally appeared, His presence was met with an unbelieving and skeptical eye. As they say, hindsight is always 20/20, and it is easy for me to point out the obvious scriptural references to the Messiah, but for the Israelites, a development like this would have been certain to shake the very core of their cultural and religious beliefs. Additionally, the temple leaders who had worked so hard in their rise to prominence would see the power they had established slip away. It is the age-old story of the position of church leadership being used as a power-base. But before we throw stones at the Jews, a study of Christian church leadership will reveal an equally dismal record of abuses, all the way up to the present.

Before I go any further, I would like to stress the point that not everyone of Jewish descent rejected Christ. Obviously, Christ and his followers were Jewish, and I believe you'll find that true Christians have a special love and concern for the Jewish community. Most importantly, though, the eternal banquet has yet to take place, and the invitations God sent out to His people are still good; they may still choose to attend the banquet. Jesus expressed his deep longing for the descendants of Abraham to recognize Him as their Savior:

> *Matthew 23:37 "O Jerusalem, Jerusalem, you who kill the prophets and stone those sent to you, how often I have longed to gather your children together, as a hen gathers her chicks under her wings, but you were not willing."*

As a way of emphasizing how significant this "invitation" was supposed to be to the Israelites, I would like to recount a few critical moments in Israel's history, which pointed toward the coming of a Savior; and again, hindsight is always 20/20.

"God himself will provide the lamb . . ."

It is important to note that the crucifixion of Christ was not "Plan B" for salvation; it was not God's reaction to the realization that things weren't going so well down on planet earth. From Judaism's beginnings, God provided hints to His people depicting how they would one day receive eternal salvation. One of the early clues is found in the book of Genesis within the story of Abraham and Isaac. After waiting patiently and finally receiving a son (at the age of 100), Abraham is told by God to sacrifice his son as a burnt offering to the Lord. (Keep in mind that Abraham had been promised that his descendants would number as the stars, and Isaac was his only hope to see that fulfilled.)

So early the next morning, Abraham set out with Isaac, but he neglected to fill him in on the agenda for the day; otherwise, I don't think Isaac would have been so quick to carry the wood. Anyway, at some point Isaac becomes suspicious and asks, um . . .

Gen. 22:7b "The fire and wood are here . . . but where is the lamb for the burnt offering?"

And without realizing it, Abraham gives a prophecy about the coming Messiah when he replies,

Gen. 22:8a "God himself will provide the lamb for the burnt offering, my son."

As you probably know from the story, an angel of the Lord stopped Abraham from sacrificing his son, and the Lord provided a ram caught in a thicket for the sacrifice. Abraham, who would then become the father of the whole nation of Israel, was spared his only son, Isaac.

The Blood of the Lamb

Now fast-forward several hundred years to about 1446 years before *out of the mud & mire*

Christ to the time of Moses, and we find that Abraham's descendants now number about six hundred thousand men, plus women and children. Most Jews and Christians are well acquainted with the story of Moses and the Exodus, so rather than give details, I'd like to focus on the Passover tradition, which started at the time of the Exodus.

Many people know that the celebration of the Passover is meant to commemorate the time when the destroying angel of the Lord "passed over" the Israelites during the last plague of death visited on the Egyptians, which came as a result of Pharaoh's refusal to let the Israelites leave Egypt. But it didn't occur to me, until reading it in the book of Exodus, that the tradition of celebrating the Passover wasn't started by the Israelites; it was instituted by God himself before the "pass over" had even happened. All the details of how they were to celebrate it were given to Moses before the plague even began, and it became obvious that the Passover was to hold great significance in the tradition of Israel. But more importantly, God was establishing a ritual, which was to be brought to completion with the coming of the Savior.

The most significant detail about the Passover was that the Israelites were required to take some of the blood of an unblemished lamb, which they would slaughter for the Passover meal, and put it on the doorframes of their houses so that the plague would pass over them. Now, the most obvious question to me is: "Why did God bother having the Israelites put the lamb's blood on the doorframe?" Certainly, being the omniscient God, He didn't need the lamb's blood to tell Him who the true Israelites were. No, it was meant to be one more sign for the Jews that they would once again be saved by the blood of a lamb. At the time of Abraham, his first born son was spared by the blood of the ram caught in the thicket, allowing the very existence of the nation of Israel. Now, in the day of Moses, every first born son of the Israelites was saved from death by the blood of the Passover lamb.

It is extremely important to note that the lamb to be slain for

Passover was to be a lamb "without defect." (Ex. 12:5) The importance of this would be established later, once Moses was instructed by God on the regulations for sacrifice. The sacrifice needed to be perfect because it was to represent the coming Savior. The holiness and majesty of God required a perfect and unblemished sacrifice to rid the world of the wickedness and sin that entered the world through Adam, and only Christ would be able to meet such lofty standards of righteousness. Though tempted, He was without sin—regardless what silly fictional code or novel-of-the-week would like to paint him otherwise.

> *1 Peter 1:18–20 "For you know that it was not with perishable things such as silver or gold that you were redeemed from the empty way of life handed down to you from your forefathers, but **with the precious blood of Christ, a lamb without blemish or defect. He was chosen before the creation of the world,** but was revealed in these last times for your sake." (emphasis added)*

Behold, the Lamb of God!

Fast-forward, once again, about a millennium and a half to the time of Jesus, and the picture of salvation becomes complete. When John the Baptist first saw Jesus coming toward him while he was baptizing and proclaiming the coming of the Messiah, he said,

> *John 1:29 "Look, the Lamb of God, who takes away the sin of the world!"*

If you think about it, this statement doesn't make any sense unless it is a prophecy from God, since Jesus had not made known to anyone that he would have to suffer and die. The Jews were mistakenly looking for a king to reign, but instead they received a Lamb who would be slain. This declaration by John had profound significance, and its purpose was to tie together all of the prophecies pointing to the coming of a Messiah, the Savior of the Jews. But just as the prophecies also predicted, He was handed over by the very people He came to save, to be tortured and crucified.

How tragically—yet magnificently—poetic: *The only Son of the Father would become the true Passover Lamb, and only by His blood will the final eternal death "pass over" us.*

It only makes sense, then, that He was betrayed and handed over to be killed on the very night He had celebrated the Passover tradition with His disciples. It was also no accident that this took place on the first day of the "Feast of the Unleavened Bread," which is the day that it was the Jewish custom to sacrifice the Passover lamb.

The Testimony of Scripture

Countless prophecies and scriptures, from hundreds of years before Christ all the way up to his birth, were shouting, "Look! Here he is! This is the One you have been waiting for!" Every aspect of His birth, His Life and the nature of His death had been predicted through the verses of Scripture; this next passage from the book of Isaiah predicts the circumstances surrounding His birth.

> *Isaiah 7:10–14 (735 B.C.) Again the Lord spoke to Ahaz, "Ask the Lord your God for a sign, whether in the deepest depths or in the highest heights." But Ahaz said, "I will not ask; I will not put the Lord to the test." Then Isaiah said, "Hear now, you house of David! Is it not enough to try the patience of men? Will you try the patience of my God also? Therefore the Lord himself will give you a sign:* **The virgin will be with child and will give birth to a son, and will call him Immanuel.**" *(emphasis added)*

The Revised Guest List

Returning to the wedding parable, this is where *we* enter the picture. Once the Israelites rejected Christ, the invitations were sent out to those who were not of Jewish descent, better known as Gentiles. At the time of Jesus, it was unheard of for someone who was Jewish to associate with an impure, godless Gentile, so for a Gentile to receive the same offer of salvation was an unforgivable offense. Even the apostle Peter, one of the first Jewish Christians and a patriarch of the early Church, struggled with the idea of Jesus pouring out His Holy Spirit on the Gentiles.

> *Acts 10:15, 27–28, 34–35, 44–46 The voice spoke to him a second time, "Do not call anything impure that God has made clean."*
>
> *. . . Talking with him (Cornelius), Peter went inside and found a large gathering of people. He said to them: "You are well aware that it is against our law for a Jew to associate with a Gentile or visit him. But God has shown me that I should not call any man impure or unclean . . .*
>
> *. . . **I now realize how true it is that God does not show favoritism, but accepts men from every nation who fear him and do what is right.*** *" (emphasis added)*
>
> *. . . While Peter was still speaking these words, the Holy Spirit came on all who heard the message. The circumcised believers who had come with Peter were astonished that the gift of the Holy Spirit had been poured out even on the Gentiles. For they heard them speaking in tongues and praising God.*

The Wedding Garment

The portion of the parable that I believe holds great significance for the modern Church is the section dealing with the improperly dressed guest. It sounds rather heartless to throw somebody out just because of his attire, but if you take it within the context of a parable about salvation, it begins to make sense.

It is believed that at the time of Jesus wedding guests were provided with a wedding garment by the family; if one of the guests were to refuse to wear it, it would be considered an insult to the family. The poorly dressed guest would have had to make a decision not to wear the garment, which is what led to the decision to throw him out, where there would be "weeping and gnashing of teeth." The wording here is significant because it is used frequently throughout the Bible to describe the eternal pain of Hell. Obviously, this person went to Hell for not wearing the wedding garment.

The Garment of Righteousness

The wedding garment, which represents the garment of righteousness provided by the Father through the death of His Son, is necessary for entry into heaven. It may seem unfair, or outdated, or closed-minded, but it is a reality the modern Church needs to come to terms with. Earlier, I pointed out that it is not unusual to hear people say things like, "Aren't we all really searching for God in our own way? Why can't there be many ways to God? If I choose to find him in nature, what business is that of yours? Who are *we* to say who goes to heaven and who doesn't?"

I believe that the improperly dressed guest would have asked similar questions. Before the king entered the room, he could very well have convinced several other guests that they were in no position to make judgments about his attire, and he may have been right. But don't you think the other guests should have done everything within their power to get him to put the garment on anyway, even while being accused of being narrow-minded? Sometimes devout Christians need to assume the role of the fellow wedding guests who have noticed many people not wearing their garments.

Only Jesus truly knows the eternal condition of each person's heart, but if this book were to help keep even one person from being tossed out of the eternal banquet, all of the time invested in it would have been worth it. The parable ends with the words, "For many are invited, but few are chosen." With that in mind, I would like to examine what Scripture says about how we can be sure that we are among the few that are "chosen."

A Righteousness from Christ

Having been involved in various types of ministry, I have found there is still a large percentage of people who believe that in order to get to heaven, they must in some way earn the right to be there, based on their performance here on earth. In other words, they need to sort of knit themselves a garment of righteousness out of the yarn of good works. But then the obvious question is, "How much is enough?" What if you can't knit to save your life, or what if the King shows up and you have only finished one sleeve? Scripture makes it very plain over and over again that it is not within our power to provide for ourselves a garment of righteousness by observing the commandments or "the law."

> *Romans 3:20–25 "Therefore no one will be declared righteous in his sight by observing the law (the scriptures); rather, through the law we become conscious of sin. But now a righteousness from God, apart from the law, has been made known, to which the Law and the Prophets testify. This righteousness from God comes through faith in Jesus Christ to all who believe. There is no difference, **for all have sinned and fall short of the glory of God,** and are justified freely by his grace through the redemption that came by Christ Jesus. God presented him as a sacrifice of atonement, through faith in his blood." (emphasis added)*

Regardless of how good we try to be, we all "fall short of the glory of God." This is why the only garment of righteousness that is acceptable to God is the one which "comes through faith in Jesus Christ to all who believe." If someone were to come up to you and say, "I want you to have this new house I just built, but only if you agree to accept it for free. If you try to pay me for it, I'll give it to someone else." The right response to this type of offer seems obvious. But for some reason, when Christ offers salvation on similar terms, there are those who still respond, "There must be a catch. I refuse to accept anything for free. I've worked hard all my life, and I'm not going to start taking charity now."

Salvation for all humanity came at a great price—through the torture and death of the innocent Son of God. The least we could do is accept the gift of eternal life without cheapening it by trying to add something to it. If right now you sense in the deepest part of your soul that what I am saying is true, then this is your wedding invitation; surrender your heart to Him and let Him purify you the way He did me. No matter what Christian denomination you belong to, salvation always requires an action of the will. No one can put the garment on for you; you must do it yourself. Even in the denominations that baptize at birth, it is done with the understanding that when you reach an age of accountability you will reaffirm that decision of your parents by saying, "Yes, I do believe in Christ and accept His sacrifice as payment for my sins. I repent of the sin in my heart and ask Him to purify me by his blood." It is not enough to have mindlessly repeated some version of those words at a church service at some point. You must have a conversion of the heart along with a confession of the lips before you are assured of salvation.

> *Romans 10:9, 13 "Because if you confess with your lips that Jesus is Lord and believe in your heart that God raised him from the dead,* **you will be saved** *. . . For everyone who calls upon the name of the Lord* **will be saved.***" (emphasis added)*

Does it sound too good to be true? Yes. Does that make it any less true? No. To simply adhere to a certain set of rules or religious rituals would be to entirely miss the purpose of Christ's sacrifice. It is not the role of organized religion to provide salvation for a person's soul, but its role is to be one of the primary vessels by which the Gospel is preached. For example, you may have heard the Gospel message countless times at church and various places without ever hearing the voice of God say, "Come, follow me." Then at some point, He speaks to your heart and gives you an invitation to the heavenly banquet, and you respond, and suddenly all that religion begins to take on an eternal significance.

Just to clarify, I have no desire to minimize the role of the organized Church; Christ himself established the Church, and it would be extremely arrogant for me to begin preaching, "Down with organized religion!" Nor do I want to say that all ritual is pointless. Christ was very careful to observe the traditions and rituals of the Jewish Sabbath, as long as they were not in contradiction to a higher principle. For example, He was ridiculed by the Church leaders for healing on the Sabbath. But He was also careful to point out that *He* was the "Lord of the Sabbath," so it was His prerogative to establish the higher good.

The Great Surrender

There is really no way to adequately express the freedom a person experiences when he or she finally reaches the point of surrender and says, "I give up trying to do it on my own, Lord. Only you can purify this sinful heart and save me." Many people sense the weight of the world lifted from their shoulders, while others might experience a cleansing of the mind and soul. Still others might be miraculously healed of an addiction or a destructive habit. I can only speak from personal experience, but rather than cause dismay or embarrass my relatives, I'll put my testimony in the form of a short story.

No Joy in Sewerville

Not too long ago, in a place too close to home, there lived a young man of about 19 years of age, who for the purposes of this story, we'll call Bob. Bob was a rebel without a clue who was going nowhere fast, slowed down only occasionally by the flickering of red and blue lights. (Since "brevity is the soul of wit," "Bob" herein will be replaced with the much shorter "I.") I lived in a wasteland called Sewerville that was flowing with sour milk and bitter honeys. Sewerville was a land below the street, and though it wasn't much, I called it home. I had everything I needed: a roof over my head, lots of people I called "friends," and a steady flow of sewage day and night that my friends and I could enjoy at our leisure.

We would spend countless hours on the warm summer days wading through the sewage looking for little treasures we could collect and put into bags along the edge of the stream. Some had more than others, but I was quite proud of my growing collection. Those who had the greatest number of treasures were idolized by the rest of us.

There were two mentors, in particular, we all admired; the first was a bitter honey, named Holly Woods. She was sweet at first, but became bitter as she got older. She had more trash than any of us could ever dream of having, but she still seemed to have a genuine interest in each of our lives.

The other idol for us was a man named Hughe Flynt. We always went to him for advice on personal issues. He seemed to have an honest desire for us to just be free and to enjoy our lives in Sewerville.

So, such was life in the wasteland called Sewerville. We spent our days laughing and sloshing around in the sewage and collecting our treasures. It was a simple life, but it was a fragrant life. We all seemed happy, but it was a horrible thing when night fell. Even in Sewerville, with all of our friends, the darkness and the loneliness of night was unbearable. I thought for sure if I could just collect enough treasures that they would keep me warm and safe at night, but it was to no avail.

The only comfort from the darkness of night was "The Being" that lived above the street.

Holly liked to refer to Him as the "Extreme Being" and she told us that He only existed in our imagination. But she encouraged us to indulge our imagination if it helped us cope. (For someone who didn't believe in Him, it always confused me to see her celebrate His birthday year after year by hanging lights and puffy little red guys around the sewer.)

Each night, under the cover of darkness, she would tell us ghost stories about how this mysterious Being would reach down through the sewer grate with His bloody pierced hand and snatch his victims from their beds *by the side of the stream. As he yanked them through the grate, He would be ramming a black book down their throats and they would be gasping and choking and fighting for air. And then they were gone . . . never to be seen again.*

Deep down, I knew that Holly Woods was embellishing the story a little because every time I saw this Being, real or imaginary, He was extending His hand to me, gently calling me to take hold of it. There was a deep longing in His eyes for me to be with Him.

But Holly's apparent wisdom always won me over. There was so much of the sewer I hadn't yet explored, and she and Hughe seemed so willing to take me there. Besides, I had collected so many treasures that it would take both hands and a few friends to get them anywhere. One time, I seem to recall (though it may have been a dream) this loving Being from above calling out to me, and I wanted so much to run to Him, but when I turned to grab my treasures, He disappeared. I tried to run after Him, but I had too much to carry and no one to help me. The despair was overwhelming and I sat, and I wept.

As I recalled that moment in my mind, I made a decision to find out for myself if this mysterious, yet loving Being really existed. When Holly and Hughe were not around, I began to ask questions, searching for the truth. As legend would have it, His physical appearance consisted of part Lion, part Lamb, and part human, and all who reached out to Him would be pulled out of the sewer into a land filled with light and true treasure beyond belief.

He would take them on a journey to a castle owned by His Father, and His Father would hold a banquet and adopt them as His sons and daughters. And there would be no more dark nights to suffer through; no more pain nor anguish nor despair.

I was told that there would be guides along the trail who would help us stay on the path, if we were willing, and then it all began to make sense to me. I suddenly realized that I had been living with two guides for the first 18 years of my life. I thought they were stalkers, because they kept trying to get close to me to steal my stuff; that's why I fled to this pungent life of sewage. When I asked Holly about them, she told me, although they were well intentioned, they were bumbling idiots when it came to understanding the real world of Sewerville.

So there I sat, surrounded by sewage, getting swept further and further down stream, closer and closer to where all sewage goes. Holly said I would end up at the castle either way, and Hughe wanted me to enjoy the ride, but I was beginning to doubt their wisdom.

I couldn't even stop to enjoy my treasures any more because the flow was carrying me too quickly to gain control. My life consisted of waste and I knew it. If I saw that mysterious Being again, would he want me? I was filthy; surely His Father had no use for me. I started to weep, and I blamed the tour guides, and I blamed Holly and Hughe, and I even blamed an artist formerly known as Princess. And then it happened…up ahead…I saw a light…and a pierced hand…and there was His voice…somehow I knew it was Him, beckoning me to grab His hand. And I begged and pleaded with Him "Please take me, I know I am dirty," and He said to me, "Just take my hand and you will be pure." As I approached Him, I tried to fix my hair and wipe away the slime to make myself presentable for this banquet, and I pleaded some more, and then I gave up the struggle and went under.

> *Psalm 69:1–3 "Save me, O God, for the waters have come up to my neck. I sink in the miry depths, where there is no foothold. I have come into the deep waters; the floods engulf me. I am worn out calling for help; my throat is parched."*

With one last gasp, I reached my hand above the sewage and I felt it—the purifying hand of God. He firmly took hold of my hand and pulled me out of the sewage, and then he stood there for what seemed like an eternity holding me in His arms. His tears of joy washed over me and purified me and made me clean. He gave me a brilliant white robe to wear to the banquet and said, "Come, follow Me."

> *Psalm 18:16 "He reached down from on high and took hold of me; He drew me out of the deep waters."*

*Psalm 40:2–3 "He lifted me out of the slimy pit, **out of the mud and mire**; He set my feet on a rock and gave me a firm place to stand. He put a new song in my mouth, a hymn of praise to our God." (emphasis added)*

If today, you hear His voice . . .

If you have even the slightest doubt that you truly belong to Jesus Christ, but you have a deep desire to grab hold of His hand and be cleansed of your past the way I was, then this could be the voice of God issuing your invitation. Psalm 95:7–8 says,

"Today, if you hear His voice, do not harden your hearts . . ."

At the age of nineteen at a weekend retreat, I remember distinctly hearing God speak to my heart and say, "Either you lose your 'cool' or you lose your eternal inheritance. The choice is yours." It was time for me to respond to His voice, but it was clear that my desire to be perceived as "cool" was hardening my heart and keeping me from responding to Him. I should explain, at nineteen, I was scared to death of becoming a blubbering heap of emotions, so I was resisting with everything I had. Fortunately, by His grace, I accepted Him that day, and the rest is interesting history. Many battles remained to be fought, but it was a foundation on which Christ could build—a foundation of grace.

If you haven't already, give your life to Him; you'll be amazed at how incredibly valuable you are to the Father and how he can make your life count from this point forward.

John 3:16–18 "For God so loved the world that he gave his one and only Son, that whoever believes in him shall not perish but have eternal life. For God did not send his Son into the world to condemn the world, but to save the world through him. Whoever believes in him is not condemned, but whoever does not believe stands condemned already because he has not believed in the name of God's one and only Son." - Jesus

The Way Forward

At the risk of over-simplifying the Christian life, I would like to compare the moment of conversion to a child who receives a new puzzle for his birthday. It comes neatly packaged in a shiny new box with the image of Christ on the front. Often, we are handed this new box at Baptism, or at a conference or retreat, and like an excited child on his birthday, we rush home and tear into the box just to find out that it is a four million piece puzzle. The concept is simple enough; just put the puzzle pieces together, but the working out of that concept—in the everyday Christian life—seems altogether overwhelming. At this point, many new Christians throw the puzzle in the trash and go back to their old lives. "Sure, it's not a beautiful portrait of Christ, but at least it is familiar and the pieces are a lot bigger."

In *The Parable of the Sower*, Jesus warns us that once we have heard the "message about the kingdom," or the Gospel message presented in this chapter, the ability for that seed of truth to take root and bear fruit in our lives will be met with many challenges. Most people are somewhat familiar with the parable, but for those who are not, I'll quote the passage:

> *Matthew 13:3–9 "A farmer went out to sow his seed. As he was scattering his seed, some fell along the path, and the birds came and ate it up. Some fell on rocky places, where it did not have much soil. It sprang up quickly, because the soil was shallow. But when the sun came up, the plants were scorched, and they withered because they had no root. Other seed fell among thorns, which grew up and choked the plants. Still other seed fell on good soil, where it produced a crop—a hundred, sixty or thirty times what was sown. He who has ears, let him hear."*

Later in the same chapter (v. 19), Jesus explains the parable to

His disciples. Paraphrasing, the seed (or the Gospel message) that fell along the path was snatched away by "the evil one" because the person hearing the Gospel lacked understanding. Hopefully this chapter has provided enough foundational understanding—regarding the necessity and purpose of the sacrifice of Christ—to help prevent the message from being snatched away. But even so, there are two other schemes of the evil one waiting in the wings:

> *Mt. 13:20–22 "The one who received the seed that fell on rocky places is the man who hears the word and at once receives it with joy. But since he has no root, he lasts only a short time. When trouble or persecution comes because of the word, he quickly falls away. The one who received the seed that fell among the thorns is the man who hears the word, but the worries of this life and the deceitfulness of wealth choke it, making it unfruitful."*

In reference to the seed that fell on rocky places, I can assure you, trouble *and* persecution are right around the corner for those who accept Christ and are willing to stand for what they believe. The book of Revelation serves as a reminder of the battle being waged in the spiritual realms against the faithful:

> *Rev. 12:17 "Then the dragon was enraged at the woman and went off to make war against the rest of her offspring—those who obey God's commandments and hold to the testimony of Jesus."*

This same point is underscored in *2 Timothy 3:12–13*,

> *"In fact, everyone who wants to live a godly life in Christ Jesus will be persecuted, while evil men and impostors will go from bad to worse, deceiving and being deceived."*

So as Christians, we should not be filled with shock and awe when the modern culture does not welcome the Christian way of life with open arms.

Returning to the *Parable of the Sower*, the battle against God's people described above is represented by the scorching sun, and those without roots will not be able to withstand it. Inspired books and teaching might act as a fertilizer for the soil, but the roots will only start to grow when all that knowledge is applied in real life circumstances. Each time we choose to defend our faith or we choose to obey the voice of God, roots begin to grow deeper and deeper into the soil, and eventually our lives become firmly planted, bearing fruit "a hundred, sixty or thirty times what was sown."

Finally, regarding the seed that fell among the thorns, the last section of this book deals with the topic of leaving a legacy by devoting our talents and resources to the service of God. In this great country of affluence, a significant number of people will have the Gospel choked out of their lives by the "worries of this life and the deceitfulness of wealth." My intention will be to help put these things into perspective, but again, it is a lot easier to write about it than to put it into practice.

The whole lesson Jesus is teaching us through this parable is that safeguarding the spiritual seed we have been entrusted with will require both spiritual understanding and an action of the will, or a spiritual battle. The remainder of this first section will be devoted to outlining the basics of the Christian faith and to outfitting ourselves with armor necessary to fight this cultural battle in which we find ourselves.

> *Rev. 12:11 "They overcame him (Satan) by the blood of the Lamb and by the word of their testimony; they did not love their lives so much as to shrink from death."*

CHAPTER 4
a lamp, a sword and a stream

". . . the Sword of the Spirit, which is the Word of God . . ."

Flawless

Psalm 12:6 And the words of the Lord are flawless, like silver refined in a furnace of clay, purified seven times.

A crucial step in the maturity process of every Christian is the point at which they must decide for themselves whether or not they believe that the Bible is the perfect, "flawless" Word of God. To leave open the option for human error will ultimately invalidate all of Scripture. Very simply, if the omnipotent, omniscient God who created the heavens and the earth and who spoke all of creation into existence is unable to dictate His Word to the beings He created, then He is no god at all. He is a product of the overactive imagination of many scholars involved in the most intricately woven, carefully preserved scam of all time. This conspiracy took thousands of years to bring to completion, but due to the dedication of those involved, the secret was preserved through generations of turmoil and strife—climaxing with the torture and death of one man for the sole purpose of securing the heritage of his family as the official bloodline of the Savior of the world.

Do you see the conflict here? Either God is God, or He is not. Either Scripture is the flawless Word of God or it is a cruel and heartless joke. It is impossible to be a disciple of Christ, while at the same time discarding the portions of Scripture that are difficult to understand or appear to contain contradictions.

Don't misunderstand, there certainly are modern "translations" not widely accepted by the Christian body, which are inherently flawed, because the motives of the editors had more to do with softening the edges for modern consumption than staying true to the Word of God. So Christians need to steer clear of translations with any other stated or implied purpose beyond accurately and faithfully interpreting the Word of God.

Obviously, the publishers of an unfaithful translation will not include in the preface, "We intend to distort and water-down the Gospel to the point where it no longer even slightly resembles the original manuscripts, but it *does* make you feel happy and warm." But just as we trusted the early Church leaders to write the books of the Bible through the guidance of the Holy Spirit, we must trust modern Church leadership to point us toward the faithful translations.

Having said that, we can take great comfort in the fact that the translations being used by the majority of Christians today are amazingly consistent. The message of the Gospel has not changed, and there is enough original manuscript evidence to keep it from ever changing. Anticipating the future arguments about accuracy, Christ shares his opinion on the likelihood of the Word of God being altered in any way:

Luke 16:17 "It is easier for heaven and earth to disappear than for the least stroke of a pen to drop out of the Law." - Jesus

Our interpretation of God's Law has no bearing on the Law itself, and as long as there are faithful men and women seeking His truth, there will be faithful Bible translations made available through the power of His Spirit. But *The* Law, or the Word of God, will always exist in Spirit form—long after the earth disappears into a cloud of dust.

Out of Context

By expressing confidence in the Word of God, I do not mean

to imply that it is impossible to take Scripture out of context. For example, if someone wanted to use Scripture for political purposes and was determined to prove that God is a Republican, he might quote Ecclesiastes 10:2,

> *"The heart of the wise inclines to the right, but the heart of the fool to the left."*

Or if someone wanted to start a cult that restricted the wearing of shorts by men, you might quote Psalm 147:10,

> *"His pleasure is not in the strength of the horse, nor his delight in the legs of a man . . ."*

Before I drift too far away from anything useful, I'd like to point out that Satan himself used the tactic of taking Scripture out of context while tempting Jesus, but Jesus rebuked him by putting the Scripture verse into perspective:

> *Matthew 4:5–7 Then the devil took him to the holy city and had him stand on the highest point of the temple. "If you are the Son of God," he said, "throw yourself down. For it is written: 'He will command his angels concerning you, and they will lift you up in their hands, so that you will not strike your foot against a stone.'" Jesus answered him, "It is also written: 'Do not put the Lord your God to the test.' "*

So to avoid misinterpretation, Scripture must be read with the wisdom of the Spirit of Christ. Psalm 111:10 explains,

> *"The fear of the Lord is the beginning of wisdom; all who follow his precepts have good understanding. To him belongs eternal praise."*

In other words, each of us needs to approach the Author of Scripture with a spirit of humility, reverence and awe, or "fear." In this "fear" we find the "beginning of wisdom," which allows us to know

His precepts, and as we follow them, we gain "good understanding." In that spirit of humility, the Psalmist prays,

> *Psalm 119:18–20 "Open my eyes that I may see wonderful things in your law. I am a stranger on earth; do not hide your commands from me. My soul is consumed with longing for your laws at all times."*

Just hearing such passion and humility toward the Word of God should inspire us to spend the time necessary in Scripture study to dispel any lingering doubts about its validity or accuracy. When I read the passages above, I'm not hearing, "Gee, I think Scripture is kinda neat, but I'm keeping an open mind in case I read a book debunking the whole thing." To be honest, I believe that the people with the most to say about the Bible's "inaccuracies" have spent the least amount of time studying it.

Scripture on Scripture?

I realize it is not exactly a scientific approach to use Scripture to prove the validity of Scripture, but that is not my intent, anyway. My point is that the belief in Scripture as the flawless Word of God is an issue of the heart, and to treat the Word of God like a smorgasbord is not an option. We must take the Brussels sprouts and lima beans along with the pudding and cake. Ultimately, we will see that the Brussels sprout portions of Scripture are good for us, and I have it on good authority that there will be no lima beans in heaven.

> *Psalm 18:30 As for God, his way is perfect; the word of the Lord is flawless.*

> *2 Timothy 3:16* **All** *scripture is God-breathed . . . (emphasis added)*

Weightlessness

To reach the point of accepting all Scripture as the Word of God is much like the transition from running a race with 100 lb. ankle weights to removing them and feeling weightless. Yes, its Author requires that we run the course that is laid out for us, but this very course also allows us to embrace the promises of Scripture as our own so that we might finish the race valiantly.

> *1 Corinthians 9:24–27 "Run in such a way as to get the prize. Everyone who competes in the games goes into strict training. They do it to get a crown that will not last;* **but we do it to get a crown that will last forever.** *Therefore I do not run like a man running aimlessly; I do not fight like a man beating the air. No, I beat my body and make it my slave so that after I have preached to others, I myself will not be disqualified for the prize." (emphasis added)*

A Lamp

> *Ps. 119:105 Your word is a lamp to my feet and a light for my path.*

I once heard a Christian teacher say that the lamp referred to in this passage is not a floodlight but a small lamp just bright enough to illuminate the ground in front of us, revealing just enough of the path to guide our next step. This is a difficult aspect of God's character for those of us—I mean those of you—who tend to be slightly impatient when seeking God's will. We want to know the whole plan, and we "want it on our desks by yesterday," but God, in his compassion, spares us. In theory, we would probably all agree that to see our life at a glance would be too much for any one of us to handle, but in actuality, we tend to respond like spoiled children when God limits our ability to see beyond the path. On the brighter side, God is also probably limiting our view of all the wolves lurking in the forest just outside the path, but as long as we keep the lamp in our hands, the wolves are more likely to avoid the light.

> *John 3:19–20 This is the verdict: Light has come into the world, but men loved darkness instead of the light because their deeds were evil. Everyone who does evil hates the light, and will not come into the light for fear that his evil deeds will be exposed.*

Each time you open the pages of the Bible, just picture the pack of wolves that was closing in on you—the fear, the guilt, the sin, the despair, the indecision—scampering into hiding as the Spirit of God streams forth from the Lamp. Attempting to live a Christian life that is pleasing to God without spending time in the Word of God is much like attempting—without a lamp—to make your way through a thick, dark forest filled with ravenous wolves seeking "someone to devour."

> *Matthew 10:16 I am sending you out like sheep among the wolves. Therefore be shrewd as snakes and as innocent as doves.*

A Sword

> *Hebrews 4:12–13 For the word of God is living and active. Sharper than any double-edged sword, it penetrates even to dividing soul and spirit, joints and marrow; it judges the thoughts and attitudes of the heart. Nothing in all creation is hidden from God's sight. Everything is uncovered and laid bare before the eyes of him to whom we must give account.*

The analogy of the sword in this passage is one of the most powerful in all of Scripture, and rightly so, because Scripture has a way of piercing right through all of our defenses and inhibitions to get right through to the "thoughts and attitudes of the heart." "Everything is laid bare" before the almighty God. What more is there to say? As we open the pages of Scripture, it is as if the pages of our heart are interwoven with Scripture—almost as if Scripture was written with our particular circumstances in mind—because it was. *That* is the mystery of Scripture. Somehow it was written in such a way as to address every possible scenario and life circumstance of every believer in all of time. "Such knowledge is too wonderful for me, too lofty for me to attain." - *Psalm 139:6*

Returning to the analogy of the forest, as the lamp lights the path, the sword (The Sword of the Spirit) is used as a weapon against the repeated attacks of the wolves brave enough to venture into the light. Christ gave an example of this as he was tempted in the desert. Satan would lunge at him with a temptation, and Christ would wield the sword of Scripture by beginning each counter attack with, "It is written." In a future chapter entitled "If God is For Us . . ." we will take a closer look at this strategy.

Living and Active

When the Word of God is described as being "living and active… sharper than any double-edged sword," usually the reader focuses in on the "sword," but it is the "living and active" that makes the sword so sharp. "Living and active" does not mean "exciting and fun to read." It literally means that Scripture is alive through the power of the Holy Spirit. Scripture and Christ are considered to be one and the same.

> *John 1:1, 14 In the beginning was the Word, and the Word was with God, and the Word was God . . . The word became flesh and made his dwelling among us. We have seen his glory, the glory of the One and Only, who came from the Father, full of grace and truth.*

In a way, Scripture could be considered the first form of interactive media known to mankind. It is not virtual reality; it *is* reality. When a child of God humbly comes before Him by reading and studying and searching His Word, the Holy Spirit opens the reader's eyes and heart to the interpretation of Scripture. There are countless examples in the scriptures where the understanding of a person was limited because of his hardness of heart or lack of faith; the Scribes and Pharisees are prime examples.

A Stream

> Psalm 1:2–3 *But his delight is in the law of the Lord, and on his law he meditates day and night.* **He is like a tree planted by streams of water,** *which yields its fruit in season and whose leaf does not wither.* **Whatever he does prospers.** *(emphasis added)*

This verse is perfect for pointing out our need to be planted by the life-giving streams of Scripture. A Christian who is firmly rooted by these streams will yield fruit worthy of the name and sacrifice of Christ. But unfortunately, all too often we try to survive without the Word of God. As a result, we might not necessarily abandon Christianity, but we will become like cacti in a desert, trying to survive on the reserves of past experiences or the occasional refreshment of a Spirit-filled retreat.

The Christian cactus can be a real source of significant irritation to those who are unfortunate enough to come into contact with him. It is difficult to comfort or to teach a cactus because of his lack of knowledge and understanding of the ways of God. For example, while I was in high school I kept a mental list of all the people I was going to get even with when I became rich and powerful. But as I grew in my relationship with Christ and began diligently studying His Word, I learned more about His love, forgiveness, and sacrifice, and that bitterness from high school was taken from me.

Scripture also serves as a refreshing stream when life itself becomes a barren desert. God's Word makes no attempt to hide the very real suffering of actual living, breathing servants of God—even the Son of God himself—but it also provides the refreshing spiritual water necessary to carry us through the sun-scorched sands of pain and suffering.

> *Psalm 22:1 "My God, my God, why have you forsaken me?"*

*Psalm 23:1–3 "The Lord is my shepherd, I shall not be in want. He makes me lie down in green pastures, **he leads me beside quiet waters, he restores my soul.**" (emphasis added)*

Ultimately, the Word of God serves as just a taste of our eternal destiny.

Revelation 7:16–17 Never again will they hunger; never again will they thirst. The sun will not beat upon them, nor any scorching heat. For the Lamb at the center of the throne will be their shepherd; he will lead them to springs of living water. And God will wipe away every tear from their eyes.

I want my life to bear fruit for the kingdom of God, so I must make every effort to stay rooted "by streams of water." I choose to cling desperately to the promises of Psalm 1 and Rev. 7.

Scripture at a Glance

The attributes of Scripture—and of Christ himself—are best described in Psalm 19. The breathtaking nature of this passage is enough to warrant an entire book in itself, but for now, I'll let the verses speak for themselves.

Psalm 19:7–11
The **Law** of the Lord is **perfect**, *reviving the soul.*
The **Statutes** of the Lord are **trustworthy**, *making wise the simple.*
The **Precepts** of the Lord are **right**, *giving Joy to the heart.*
The **Commands** of the Lord are **radiant**, *giving light to the eyes.*
The **Fear of the Lord** is **pure**, *enduring forever.*
The **Ordinances** of the Lord are **sure** and altogether **righteous**.
They are more **precious** than gold, than much pure gold; they are **sweeter than honey**, than honey from the comb.

By them *your servant is warned; in keeping them there is great reward.* (Italics and bold emphasis added)

The Reward

As I said in the beginning of this chapter, there is an incredible sense of freedom that comes with accepting Scripture as the pure and divinely inspired Word of God. Once I finally decided to make it a priority to spend time in the scriptures every day, my faith began to grow tremendously, and I can say without any doubt that Scripture study has been an anchor through some difficult times.

In some ways, it takes a great act of faith to believe that every single one of the countless contributors to the Bible was divinely inspired. But the more familiar you become with Scripture as a whole, the more you begin to realize how perfectly the pieces fit together. Then Scripture study becomes less of an act of faith and more of a builder of faith, and eventually, that faith becomes unshakable.

CHAPTER 5
unshakable faith

The Shield of Faith

> Luke 18:8 "However, when the Son of Man comes, will he find faith on the earth?"

Leaving Home

When our eldest son decided, after much consideration of course, that it was time for him to leave home, he packed his belongings and his sleeping bag and slowly but confidently headed for the front door. At that moment, it all began to hit us like a ton of bricks; the first step toward an empty nest, our first born son taking a step toward manhood; it was like losing a piece of our hearts.

My wife, as she is often given to worry about practical matters, proceeded to ask him how he would support himself and where he would live. It was typical of a mother about to release her child and not wanting to let go. He responded to her by saying, "Mom, you just have to have faith. Jesus will take care of me." It was precious to us; a child we had raised, clinging to his knowledge of God . . . a kind of simple faith . . . a childlike faith that would surely sustain him through the rough times.

Call it a lack of faith on our part or just simply unbelief, but we still had some nagging concerns—not the least of which was the fact that he was only six years old. But not wanting to stifle his creativity or to invade his right to individuality, we let him go and pointed him in the direction of his aunt and uncle, who live a block away. We called them and informed them of Joshua's decision to live with them, and I instructed his Uncle Sam (no relation) to put him to work—to make him earn his keep.

After about an hour or so of dusting and cleaning, Joshua had a change of heart and began to look for a chance to escape. The opportunity came when he noticed that both his aunt and uncle had gone upstairs. He seized the moment and ran for his life, leaving behind everything he had taken with him including his favorite toys. He came running through the back door, slamming it against the stove, and he embraced us like the Prodigal Son returning from his journey. He quickly forgot about whatever it was that he wasn't allowed to do that prompted his departure. Alice and I weren't sure whether to laugh or cry, but we were happy to have him back; the whole scenario had a strange feeling of reality and permanence to it. As I write, he is now a teenager and hasn't run away since.

Circumstantial Faith

In many ways, my son's flawed rationale as he left the house is very similar to the approach we take as modern Christians to our faith in the heavenly Father. For example, take a look at the false security in which my son took confidence as he prepared to leave home. He had gotten so used to the provision of his every need that he developed a false sense of security in his circumstances, giving no thought to the provider—me. Now I realize that God provides for him through me, but God teaches reliance on the Father through the father-child relationship. If this is missing in a child's life, it could be a roadblock to his faith in God later in life, and nothing short of divine intervention will be able to restore that trust. Only a single mother can truly appreciate how profoundly the absence of a father can impact a child, and only a God whose Son was murdered by the likes of us can fill that void for both of them.

So like a child who has run away, we tend to take for granted the provision of God and to assume it will always be there, regardless of how we live our lives. We make decisions based on our own human calculations, and then we ask God to stamp it with his signet ring, without giving any consideration to what *His* plan might be.

Childlike Faith

Our goal, then, is to develop a faith that is in God, Himself, and not our circumstances. When God reveals His love as a Father, we begin to understand that He has our best interests in mind—even if we don't understand our circumstances. My children don't always understand the decisions I make, but they have trust that my love for them will cause me to make the decisions that are best for them; it is a "childlike faith."

What begins to tear down this faith is the development of intellect, coupled with peer pressure (plus or minus a few hormones). Once the intellect is fully formed, amazingly at the age of 13 or 14, we begin to question everything, and suddenly that loving father and mother have changed into an evil coalition that exists solely to spoil our fun.

As a child, when we skinned our knees, we didn't question the existence of God and his goodness, and probably didn't cry out, "How could a loving God allow me to skin my knee?" But with age comes the realization that God has the ability to prevent some of the pain and suffering we experience, and suddenly resentment toward God and self-pity cause a wedge in the relationship.

Pain and Suffering

The last thing I want to do is trivialize anyone's pain and suffering in this life, and it is unlikely I will be able to adequately cover the topic in a short sub-section of one chapter. But rather than skip the topic altogether, I'll just offer a few thoughts for consideration.

It is much easier to discuss sin and the resulting consequences than it is to understand the seemingly random pain and suffering we experience in life; the cause-effect aspect of suffering is far less obvious than that of sin and consequences. There are many things in this fallen state of humanity that will fail to make any sense on this side of eternity: death, tragedy, abortion, sickness and disease, the loss of a child, poverty, and the list goes on. So rather than try to explain why these things happen, it would be more profitable for us to explore the outcome of pain and suffering, and hopefully in doing so it will become more clear to us why God allows such things to happen.

One aspect about suffering is that it causes us to take our focus away from temporal things and place it on things eternal. We are under the mistaken impression that God's sole purpose is to keep us comfortable and well fed in this life, but God's ultimate goal is that you and I spend eternity with him. If pain and suffering drive us to our knees, then pain and suffering ultimately have incalculable eternal value.

Now, I realize the last statement will be no comfort to those who are suffering, but maybe this next statement will be. We have a God who endured the worst pain and suffering known to mankind so that we might spend eternity with him. Somehow, when we are focused on him, his grace is sufficient to carry us through.

The crucifixion of Christ represents the most unjust torturing of an innocent person that has ever been known to mankind, but it is much more than that from God's perspective. For reasons beyond our ability to comprehend, our salvation hinged on one man's obedience and sacrifice, and at the time, it made sense to no one who was associated with Him. Those who believe that all pain and suffering comes as a result of un-repented sin will have a very difficult time explaining the death of Christ. No theologian or philosopher could have predicted by deduction or induction or intuition or even common sense that the salvation of this corrupt world would come as a result of the death of the Son of God. It doesn't make sense—but what a glorious reality it is.

Romans 8:18 "I consider that our present sufferings are not worth comparing with the glory that will be revealed in us."

The Antidote to Self-Sufficiency

Another aspect of pain and suffering is that it brings us back to the realization of how desperately in need we are for the heavenly Father to sustain us. Our tendency as human beings is to become reliant on our own self-sufficiency, but the reality is that this world is hopelessly out of control, and we are no more able to provide for ourselves than a child in the womb. It often takes a crisis to make us fully aware of our need for the provision and guidance of the Father.

Faith, by its very definition, must be tried, or it is not faith at all. We think God tests us in order to find out how strong our faith is, but I am discovering that trials have more to do with God revealing to us the level of faith we have; it is more for our benefit, not His. He is forming us in His image, not trying to find out what the family resemblance is.

As an example, when my wife and I were first married, we had a lot of accumulated debt as a result of poor decisions. (I say "we" because when you get married, you become one with your spouse, and you get to shift the blame to your partner. This is a very biblical concept, and I have Scripture quotes available upon request.) Our idea of a budget in our early married life was to finance what we wanted and then try to find a way to make enough money to pay for it. I was self-employed, so I—I mean we—were very self-reliant when it came to finances. We thought we were slick enough to get ourselves out of anything.

So, when the creditors started calling—every day—we stopped answering the phone. It got to the point where we hated to hear the phone ring. My pride refused to admit that we were in trouble, and I had convinced myself that it was just a matter of time before the big money started rolling in. We had a nice truck, fully loaded, on which

I received many compliments, and we at least had the appearance of being successful.

Until—on Good Friday no less—a man came to our door and asked in a somewhat forceful tone to have the keys to the truck. So on Good Friday that year, my pride was crucified with Christ. I was at the end of myself and had nothing left but the house on which to attach my pride, which I vowed never to sell because I knew it would be difficult to ever get another mortgage.

We sold the house for a nice profit, making a small dent in our debt situation, but the day we moved proved to be one of the best—and worst—days of my life. It was one of the best because my wife was in the hospital giving birth to my beautiful baby girl, Karine. But with the certainty offered through God's precious gift of life came the uncertainty of my own life, which was drowning in turmoil. I had nothing left. I had no house, no money, no truck and no pride—all of those truly important things in life—none of which I had. If that was not enough, I could not have picked a worst day to move; it was a miserable winter day with temperatures below zero, and just for good humor, I had the flu (with all of its symptoms). It has been said, "When God closes a door, he opens a window," and I was looking for a window from which to leap.

But that day, God gave me a lead on a job through a Christian friend of ours. It was a good job with good pay and good benefits, and I jumped at the opportunity. God took that shell of a man, void of any purpose or meaning, and began to fill me and form me into His image. I make light of the situation now, but at the time there was very little to laugh about. I had succeeded in hurting anyone and everyone who was close to me, but most of all, my wife Alice, who had to deal with the phone calls and threatening letters day-in and day-out while she was at home raising our children.

I should clarify, I don't consider financial difficulties to be on the same level as watching a loved one suffer from a terminal disease or the loss of a child, but to a young marriage, the suffering was real, nonetheless. Through all of this, we often wondered why God was allowing such pain in our lives, when He had the ability to change it in a heartbeat. Only now, when I look back, can I see that God was driving out of me (and still is) this tendency to trust in myself for my provision and identity. God still reminds me of this lesson from time to time, and each time I am a little less stubborn than the time before . . . I hope—I mean *we* hope!

> *Romans 5:3–5 ". . . we also rejoice in our sufferings, because we know that suffering produces perseverance; perseverance, character; and character, hope. And hope does not disappoint us, because God has poured out his love into our hearts by the Holy Spirit, whom He has given us."*

All sufferings in life will not be this obvious or as clear in their explanation, but we put our hope in the character of God and have faith in the goodness of His will. As Christ said in the Garden of Gethsemane, "My Father, if it is not possible for this cup to be taken away unless I drink it, may your will be done." (Matthew 26:42)

Faith as Righteousness

Faith is described in Hebrews 11:1 as " . . . being sure of what we hope for and certain of what we do not see." This verse does not suggest that we should have faith in our ability to hear God or in our ability to summon Him when we have needs to be met. Some of the faith movements in our society distort the Gospel and treat God more like a genie than the Creator of the universe. By His grace, He answers our prayers through faith, but He is in no way obligated to do so. A truly unshakable faith is rooted in His character, not in our ability to understand His character.

Many men and women of faith in the Bible stood firm because their eyes were focused on God. When Peter began to walk on water, he was able to do so as long as his eyes were focused on Christ. As soon as he took notice of the wind and waves, his faith was shaken and he began to sink. On the other hand, the example of Abraham was one of steadfast faith:

> *Romans 4:3, 18 "Abraham believed God, and it was credited to him as righteousness"..."Against all hope, Abraham in hope believed and so became the father of many nations..."*

According to this passage, faith is a form of righteousness. It was not Abraham's outward observance of the requirements of God's law that was "credited to him as righteousness," but his faith. I make this distinction because in chapter three, I said that no one is saved by the observance or completion of a set of traditions or rituals, but by faith in Christ.

In the book of Romans, Paul zeroes in on this theme of "Faith as Righteousness" because many of his fellow Jews were placing a supreme value on the physical act of circumcision—as opposed to the true conversion of the heart—and he viewed this as a grave mistake. Paul's intent in his letter to the Romans was to assure the Gentiles that it was possible to be saved without having observed the Jewish rite of circumcision, and he does this by showing that Abraham was justified by faith even before he was circumcised.

> *Romans 4:9b-11a, 13–15a "We have been saying that Abraham's faith was credited to him as righteousness. Under what circumstances was it credited? Was it after he was circumcised, or before? It was not after, but before! And he received the sign of circumcision, a seal of the righteousness that he had by faith while he was still uncircumcised...*
>
> *... It was not through law that Abraham and his offspring received the promise that he would be heir of the world, but through the righteousness that comes by faith. For if those who live by law are heirs, faith has no value and the promise is worthless, because law brings wrath."*

Paul used the example of Abraham to show that faith, not performance, is at the heart of our eternal destinies. His goal was not to discredit the law, but to shift our attention away from our ability—or inability—to fulfill the laws of God and point it toward the saving work of Christ. Above, he says, " . . . if those who live by the law are heirs, faith has no value . . ." So faith acquires its value for each one of us as we surrender our right to try to work our way into heaven. Should we, then, ignore the commands of God as a way of expressing faith?

Romans 3:31 "Do we, then, nullify the law by this faith? Not at all! Rather we uphold the Law."

Christ showed us through His example that the righteousness acquired by faith is brought to its proper completion through the outward observance of the Law, not unlike the sign of circumcision for the Jews. Obedience to the law of God is the outward sign of an inward change.

Matthew 3:13–15 Then Jesus came from Galilee to the Jordan to be baptized by John. But John tried to deter him, saying, "I need to be baptized by you, and do you come to me?"

Jesus replied, "Let it be so now; it is proper for us to do this to fulfill all righteousness."

Faith is *the* prerequisite to the righteousness offered by Christ, and only through faith will our lives be pleasing to God.

Hebrews 11:6 "And without faith it is impossible to please God, because anyone who comes to Him must believe that He exists and that He rewards those who earnestly seek Him."

How Do I Know If I Have Faith?

So if faith is necessary to please God, how can each of us honestly assess this area of our spiritual journey? Well, first and foremost, every one of us who has chosen to accept the atoning death of Christ as payment for our sins is off to a good start; this requires a supreme act of faith. But faith is something that should continue to grow and strengthen as we mature in our relationship to God, and one look at our life decisions will speak volumes about the maturity of our faith. We often marvel at the faith (or stupidity) of the person in the circus who is the assistant to the knife thrower. He or she stands still against a board as the master throws razor sharp knives, outlining the assistant's body with great precision. The audience applauds and shows great faith in the knife thrower, but is it really faith, or is it hopeful optimism? One way to find out is to ask for a volunteer to play the part of the assistant. Suddenly, I believe you will find out how much faith there really is in the audience.

Now, this is not a perfect analogy because God is not in the business of getting us as close as possible to danger to see if we'll flinch. But it works from the standpoint that many of us proclaim great faith in the Lord until he asks us to put our lives and our decisions into his hands. Then, all of a sudden our applause for His greatness goes quiet, and we sneak out the back door with the shameful realization that we don't trust Him at all. A person of great faith is one who believes in the character of God regardless of the external circumstances, and one who obeys the voice of God without reservation. But the question still is: "Where does this type of faith come from?"

The Fatherhood of God

1 John 3:1 "How great is the love the Father has lavished on us, that we should be called children of God."

One important element of faith is the life of prayer that supports it, and to understand prayer we must first address the question of why God bothers listening to us at all. In Andrew Murray's book *With Christ in the School of Prayer*, he states, "The secret of prayer in spirit and truth is in the knowledge of the fatherhood of God, the revelation of His infinite fatherliness in our hearts, and the faith in His infinite love of us as His children." He goes on to say, "To have Christ the Son, and the Spirit of the Son dwelling within us and revealing the Father makes us true spiritual worshippers."

I will be addressing the topic of prayer later in the book, but for the purposes of this chapter, suffice it to say that if getting to know God as *Father* is crucial to a life of prayer, than it is equally crucial to forming an unshakable faith. It is no small coincidence that the crisis of faith in our country is accompanied by a deterioration of the role of the natural father in families around the globe. As a result of the fallen state of humanity, our first glimpse into the character of God is flawed because it comes through the father-child relationship. It is no wonder that we often view the Heavenly Father in the same way we view our earthly father. For example, if a child has been abandoned, abused, or neglected by his or her biological father, the pain and heartache might carry over into a mistrust or even hatred of the Heavenly Father.

As I look into the eyes of my own children, I begin to understand why God chose the father-child relationship as a standard for our relationship with Him. Since we are quite limited in our knowledge of the Creator, eternal life, the soul, the Spirit, and His love for us, God chose the father-child relationship to help explain all of this in terms we could understand as fallen human beings. I don't understand the dynamics of why I love my children so much and why I would give my life for them, but my inability to understand this type of sacrificial love does not negate its existence. Furthermore, I understand even less the abandonment of an earthly father and the intense pain and anguish and suffering that must follow, but those who have known this level of pain and anguish firsthand possess an insight to the crucifixion that I will never be able to fully comprehend.

I am not attempting to put a positive spin on the neglect of an earthly father, but to draw attention to an aspect of the Cross that is often overlooked. It is my belief that for Christ, what was more painful than the abandonment of friends, the spitting and mocking, the lashing of the whip, the weight of the cross, the crown of thorns cutting into His skull or the piercing of the nails into his hands and feet, was the feeling of abandonment by the Father that he experienced as the sins of the world were placed on His shoulders. "My God, my God . . . why have you forsaken me?" (Mt. 27:46)

His grace was not cheap; it came at a great price, and through this price He has lavished on us the privilege of being called His sons and daughters.

At a youth retreat a few years back, I was serving as a counselor, and as I was listening to a teaching on the various aspects of God's character, God spontaneously poured out a knowledge of His love for me that caused me to weep uncontrollably. What caused this was a very simple drawing that each of us received depicting a small child reaching up to take hold of the strong and loving hand of his father. As I was staring at the picture, an incredible sense and awareness of God's Fatherly love just surrounded me as if I was being held in the palm of His hand. As I sat there with my face in my hands, I have to admit I was somewhat embarrassed; I was there as a counselor, and I saw it as my responsibility to pray with those who were too weak to control their emotions. Anyway, I discreetly made my way to the restroom and stayed there until I gained my composure, but I was forever changed in my understanding of the Fatherhood of God. More than a decade and a half later, I still carry that simple drawing with me in my Bible to remind me of what God revealed to me that day.

Once the Father divinely reveals to us through His Spirit that we are His children, it is the beginning of a truly unshakable faith in His Son, and it dispels the spirit of fear, opening the door to all other areas of Christian maturity. Then we will be able to *truly* say, "our present sufferings are not worth comparing with the glory that will be revealed in us."

> *Rom. 8:15–17* "For you did not receive a spirit that makes you a slave again to fear, but you received the Spirit of sonship. And by him we cry, 'Abba Father.' The Spirit himself testifies with

*our spirit that we are God's children. Now if we are children, then we are heirs—heirs of God and co-heirs with Christ, if indeed we share in his suffering in order **that we may also share in his glory.** I consider that our present sufferings are not worth comparing with the glory that will be revealed in us."* (emphasis added)

A faith that is built upon the revelation of the Fatherhood of God by the Spirit may then be used as a shield of protection as we engage the spiritual battles that a child of God will inevitably face.

The Shield of Faith

Ephesians 6:16 "In addition to all this, take up the shield of faith, with which you can extinguish the flaming arrows of the evil one."

The NIV Scripture concordance I use explains that the shield described in the verse above was a "Roman shield covered with leather, which could be soaked in water and used to put out flame-tipped arrows." It has been my experience that, although the shield of faith is primarily a gift from God, there are certain ways in which we are responsible for keeping the leather soaked in the water of the Holy Spirit. For example, if we go for long periods of time without studying Scripture or praying, the leather becomes dry and brittle, and it doesn't take much for the "evil one" to set it ablaze. Also, if we separate ourselves for long periods of time from the Church or from hearing God's Word, our faith is easily weakened by the "flaming arrows."

Romans 10:17 Consequently, faith comes from hearing the message, and the message is heard through the word of Christ.

So if we separate ourselves from hearing the message, our faith is hindered.

The Three Components of the Shield

At the risk of oversimplifying it, the shield of faith is made up of three major components. The first component is the shield itself, which represents the divine gift of faith necessary for us to respond to the Gospel message. It is a gift of the Holy Spirit and cannot be tainted by human failings and weaknesses.

But in order for this faith to be effective in spiritual battle, it is covered in leather, which is the second component. This leather represents the element of faith tied to our level of belief, and it consists of all the things God has put into place to make the shield effective in extinguishing the arrows of the enemy. Some examples would be the Church, prayer, Christian fellowship, worship, teaching, service, etc.

The third component is the water of the Holy Spirit, necessary for keeping the elements of our faith from developing dry rot. A faith weighed down by several layers of spiritual leather but without the drenching of the Holy Spirit ends up being just a really heavy piece of armor, likely to be thrown off to the side as the soldier becomes weary. The Holy Spirit is not only responsible for making our faith effective, but also for giving us the strength to lift the shield of faith to use it.

> *Zechariah 4:6 So he said to me, "This is the word of the Lord to Zerubbabel: 'Not by might nor by power, but by my Spirit,' says the Lord Almighty."*

Up to this point, we have studied the Helmet of Salvation, the Breastplate of Righteousness, the Sword of the Spirit, and the Shield of Faith. But in order to have a more complete understanding of how the Armor of God works together in the life of a Christian, we must gain some understanding of the power of the Holy Spirit. So in the next chapter, I will attempt to explain the unexplainable—the working of the Spirit—and I am trusting that this very same Holy Spirit will guide me in this endeavor.

CHAPTER 6
the counselor

"... I will pour out my Spirit on all people ..."

John 14:26 "But the Counselor, the Holy Spirit, whom the Father will send in my name, will teach you all things and will remind you of everything I have said to you." - Jesus

Whatever happened to the outpouring of the Holy Spirit we read about in the account of Pentecost? Why does it seem as if the Holy Spirit is always the first member of the Trinity to get filtered out as the Christian faith becomes more progressive? The answers to these questions can be rather complicated, but before I attempt to answer them, I would first like to take a look at how faith, good works, and the Holy Spirit work together.

Faith Without Works

In reality, "faith by itself, if it is not accompanied by action, is dead." (James 2:17) Again, in James 2:26 it says, "As the body without the spirit is dead, so faith without deeds is dead." This can be a little confusing, since Ephesians 2:8–9 says,

> *"For it is by grace you have been saved, through faith—and this is not from yourselves, it is the gift of God—not by works, so that no one can boast."*

This would appear to be a contradiction in Scripture, and to this day it is still a heated debate among denominations. But if you continue to read Ephesians 2:10, it begins to make more sense:

> *"For we are God's workmanship, created in Christ Jesus to do good works, which God prepared in advance for us to do."*

As I said in the last chapter, works are more of an outward indicator of our willingness to obey God and a true sign of our salvation, rather than a method of gaining salvation. Also, if we are carrying out the works we were created to do, the manifestation of this obedience will be a faith that is alive, not dead or stagnant.

Faith Renewed by the Spirit

As an illustration, our heart is similar to a pond. The moment we are saved or "born again," Jesus empties the old pond of all the filthy water and the stagnant slime, and He fills it with the fresh water of His love and salvation. For a time, we are overwhelmed by His purity and goodness, but then a green film gradually begins to form on the top of our faith and we start to realize that we must make Him *Lord*, as well as Savior. The *Savior* part was easy; just repent and accept the death of Christ as payment for our sins, and all is well. But now, the fresh water is not so fresh and clear any more; as a matter of fact, it is downright repugnant.

Then the Spirit of God speaks to us on a particular issue—it could be an issue of sin, or a relationship, or the way we treat our spouse, etc.—and the Spirit shows us that the waters of our faith are being dirtied by this sewer pipe that we are allowing to empty into our spiritual pond. At this point, we realize we have to obey the Spirit of God on this matter or live in a pond that has an unbearable stench, destroying our witness to the purity of Christ. As Christians, when we resist the Lordship of Christ, we appear to be hypocrites to those around us—and believe me, people are watching.

Sadly, the other option (which many people choose at this point) is to abandon the faith altogether and return to their old way of life—

reminding us of the words of Jesus in *The Parable of the Sower,* explained in chapter 3.

Different Types of Works

The point I was making above was that obedience to the voice of God is one type of work necessary for keeping the waters of our faith pure by removing sin from our lives. By this, we stop the flow of sewage into our pond, but there still needs to be a constant flow of fresh water to keep the pond from becoming stagnant. This is accomplished through the "good works" described in Ephesians 2:10, " . . . good works which God has prepared in advance for us to do." Devoting ourselves to these "good works" could be similar to the digging of channels leading to our pond, providing a route for the refreshing rain of the Spirit of God to renew our faith. For example, any time I have served someone else with no motive of gain for myself, I have always marveled at how refreshed and renewed I am, spiritually. *1 Timothy 3:13* says,

> *"Those who have served well gain an excellent standing and great assurance in their faith in Christ Jesus."*

I believe this is why Christ taught so frequently about service; it is crucial to the health and purity of our faith. "Faith without deeds is dead." This is why I believe it is possible to have a doctrinally sound Christian group or church with a faith that is dead or stagnant. The Author of Life knows our motivations for digging the trenches, and if our heart is right, He will rain down His Spirit and renew our faith. This next verse from James drives home the point.

> *James 1:27 "Religion that God our Father accepts as pure and faultless is this: to look after orphans and widows in their distress and to keep oneself from being polluted by the world."*

According to this verse, good works combined with personal purity is the prescription for a "pure and faultless" faith. Additionally, I believe that obedience to God—being within his will for your life—is crucial to seeing an outpouring of the Holy Spirit. For example, I could say to my wife and four children, "Honey, kids, God has called me to feed the hungry children in the tribal town of Waakalookoo. I'll be leaving tomorrow." Although this might be a noble gesture, and the children of Waakalookoo will appreciate me and make me feel good about myself, this will not revive my spiritual faith if I neglect the family he has already blessed me with.

Better Than Sacrifice

All too often, good works are used as a distraction to keep us from really examining our faith, or even worse, to offset the sin in our lives. You can be certain that the Holy Spirit will not revive the spiritual health of a wayward child of God. Good works done in disobedience will bring spiritual exhaustion.

In the book of 1 Samuel, Saul is anointed king, and the Lord instructs him to go to war against the Amalekites. He is told to destroy everything belonging to them and not to spare anything, but instead, he decides to spare their king and some of his belongings, including the best of his sheep and cattle. Then to make matters worse, when confronted by the prophet Samuel, he insists he did everything the Lord commanded. When Samuel asks, "What then is this bleating of sheep in my ears?" Saul pretends as if he kept the livestock for the purpose of offering sacrifices to the Lord. Then Samuel says to him,

> *1 Samuel 15:22–23 "Does the Lord delight in burnt offerings and sacrifices as much as in obeying the voice of the Lord? To **obey is better than sacrifice,** and to heed is better than the fat of rams. For rebellion is like the sin of divination, and arrogance like the evil of idolatry. Because you have rejected the word of the Lord, he has rejected you as king." (emphasis added)*

From that point on, King Saul's reign was a downward spiral toward paranoia and psychotic behavior, and he eventually took his own life after being injured on the battlefield. Not to overstate the point, but you can see how obeying God's voice is somewhat crucial to experiencing his blessings in our lives.

If obeying "the voice of the Lord" is so important, then we may assume that hearing his voice is a prerequisite to obeying it. It follows, as well, that He must be speaking to his children in a way that is spiritually audible. Otherwise, it would be like me saying to my daughter, "Christa, because you did not paint the house, you have fallen from grace, and I am withdrawing my favor from your bank account." At which point, she could reply, "Dearest father, with all due respect, you didn't ask me to paint the house."

God does speak to his children, and he does it through his Holy Spirit; " . . . the Counselor . . . will remind you of everything I have said to you." (Jn. 14:26)

The Burning Heart

One of my favorite stories in the Bible is from the Gospel of Luke (24:13–35), and it takes place on the day Jesus had risen from the dead. Two of Jesus' followers were on their way to a town called Emmaus, and along the way they were discussing all the things that had happened regarding Christ's crucifixion. As they were talking, Jesus came along side of them and asked, "What are you discussing together as you walk along?"

They didn't know who He was because (v. 16) "they were kept from recognizing him," so the two men proceeded to explain to Jesus everything that had happened. They told Him that the one called Jesus had been crucified, and they were hoping that He would have been the one to redeem Israel. But now they were distraught and a little confused, since some of their women had reported seeing Jesus alive and well. Then he said to them,

> *v. 25–26 "How foolish you are, and how slow of heart to believe all the prophets have spoken! Did not the Christ have to suffer these things and then enter his glory?"*

He then explained to them everything Moses and the Prophets had said concerning Himself, and they were so enthralled with Him that they asked Him to spend the evening with them.

> *v. 30–32 When he was at the table with them, he took bread, gave thanks, broke it and began to give it to them. Then their eyes were opened and they recognized him, and he disappeared from their sight. They asked each other, "Were not our hearts burning within us while he talked with us on the road and opened the Scriptures to us?"*

There are at least two significant things in the passage above regarding how we are to recognize the working of the Holy Spirit in our lives. The first is our hearts should burn as the Spirit of Christ opens the Scriptures to us and as God speaks to us. And the second is that Christ intends for our spiritual eyes to be opened as we participate in—depending on your particular denomination—the traditions or sacraments He established for us. It was no accident that His followers were kept from recognizing Him until the breaking of the bread.

The Body Without the Spirit

So returning to our original question, why is the Holy Spirit—the voice and the presence of God—the first person of the Trinity to be ejected from the faith? I'll list a few possible reasons, but the issue is quite complex, so I reserve the right to be wrong.

A Messy Business

First, in the case of denominational churches, the Holy Spirit is very difficult to box in or to package in such a way that the working of the Spirit is accounted for in a particular time slot during a service. You can't say, "Between 10:45 and 10:50 we'll leave time for the Holy Spirit to fall afresh on us." In the case of salvation you can say "Do such and such, recite thus and so, and you will be saved," so it is easier to fit salvation into a spiritual formula than the Holy Spirit. Also, it is much easier to talk about the Father and His love for us and the fact that He sent His only Son to save us, than to have faith that His Son will work miracles in our lives through the power of His Spirit.

Jesus makes this point in *Luke 5:23–25*:

> *"Which is easier to say, 'your sins are forgiven,' or to say, 'get up and walk'? But that you may know that the Son of Man has authority on earth to forgive sins . . . ' He said to the paralyzed man, 'I tell you get up, take your mat and go home."*

The less we rely on the power of the Holy Spirit in our lives or in the Church, the more we become content to say things like, "The Holy Spirit was meant for the apostolic age," or "Spiritual gifts aren't necessary for the day-to-day functioning of the church," or "You worship God your way, and I'll do it my way." We would do well to note that Christ did *not* say, "I am going away, but I will send you a Counselor who will be with you for a short time whilst you establish your spiritual feet under you. But then He must return to me, lest I be without my Spirit."

Anxiety or Fear

Another cause for the absence of the Holy Spirit is the inability to trust in something we can't see or touch or even imagine. So when life overtakes us, we begin to take notice of the wind and the waves, forgetting about whom it was that told us to "come," and we sink because of our lack of faith.

Spiritual Arrogance

In the early years of a new church or in our own spiritual journey, we have a tendency to rely on the power of the Holy Spirit to build our faith and ministries, but with spiritual and numerical growth comes arrogance. As we grow in our knowledge of God and His ways, the tendency is to take pride in our knowledge and growth, and at this point, we can be sure that the Spirit's next order of business will be spiritual humility. Christ made no attempt to hide His displeasure with the scribes and Pharisees, because their arrogance blinded not only themselves, but their followers as well. When an individual or a Christian organization gets to the point where it is peering over its spiritual bifocals at the pathetic underlings of the Christian faith, you can be sure that spiritual death is not far behind.

> *Philippians 2:5–8 "Your attitude should be the same as that of Christ Jesus: who, being in very nature God, did not consider equality with God something to be grasped, but made himself nothing, taking the very nature of a servant, being made in human likeness. And being found in appearance as a man, he humbled himself and became obedient to death—even death on a cross."*

Disobedience and Impurity

At the beginning of this chapter, we examined how disobedience and impurity affect the spirituality of an individual or congregation. It is my belief that the primary reason the modern Church does not fully experience the power of the Holy Spirit the way Christ intended is the prevalence of impurity and sin within the Church. This is a rather strong assertion, but I believe a study of Scripture on the topic will validate this point. In Chapter eight, *Muddy Waters*, I will go into greater depth on this topic.

Rotten Fruit

As the Holy Spirit ceases to work in a person's life or in the life of a church, there will be a noticeable absence of good works and evangelism, or *spiritual fruit*. Also, I am fully convinced that the lives of those within the Church should look significantly different than those outside of the Church, but unfortunately, this is not often the case.

Matthew 7:19–20 "Every tree that does not bear good fruit is cut down and thrown into the fire. Thus, by their fruit you will recognize them."

If a church is not bearing fruit, you will find they will spend lots of time on forming councils and committees and meetings about the council's approach to forming the committees, while the Gospel and worship and Christian service get buried in a sea of busyness. If I am a tree, and my owner sees that I am not bearing fruit, no amount of apologetics on the fact that I am a fruit tree will keep him from cutting me down. A church without the Spirit of God is a cemetery. It is a place where people are lured into a false sense of security and comfort about their eternal condition, never being challenged to live for their Savior. The vitality of a church depends entirely on the work of the Spirit of God, coupled with man's response.

Giving up the Ghost

I believe that the most glaring characteristic of a spiritually dead church or individual is the denial or abandonment of the power of God, the Holy Spirit. They can be recognized as "having a form of godliness but denying its power (the Holy Spirit). Have nothing to do with them." (2 Timothy 3:5)

Very often, I'll find myself more inspired by a recent convert speaking by the power of the Holy Spirit than a well educated, well traveled, well read, excellent orator, who has spent his whole life gathering knowledge about God but has never really gotten to know Him personally through His Spirit.

Job 32:8–9 "But it is the Spirit in a man, the breath of the Almighty, that gives him understanding. It is not only the old who are wise, not only the aged who understand what is right."

In Matthew 11:25–26 Jesus says,

"I praise you Father, Lord of heaven and earth, because you have hidden these things from the wise and learned, and revealed them to little children. Yes, Father, for this was your good pleasure."

My wife and I are often amazed at the wisdom that comes out of the mouths of our children. There is something about their humility and purity of heart that allows the Holy Spirit to speak to us through them.

Matthew 21:14–16 While Jesus was teaching in the temple, the children were shouting "Hosanna to the Son of David," causing the chief priests to become indignant. Jesus responds to them by saying, "Have you never read, 'From the lips of children and infants you have ordained praise'?"

It is this very same childlike humility and purity that will be necessary if we are to experience the full power of God through His Spirit.

Foolishness of the Spirit

So what should our approach be to this mysterious Being whom is so necessary, yet so seemingly elusive? It is just human nature for our first reaction to the things we don't understand to be ridicule or humor (except in the case of the humor used in this book). Humor helps us to take the edge off the uneasy feeling of inadequacy that results from our lack of knowledge or experience. Sometimes my wife will ask me a question about which I don't necessarily have all the conclusive data needed to adequately answer her with a high degree of accuracy. So my response will be something like, "If *you* don't know the answer to that, *I* certainly am not going to tell you."

At Pentecost, when the Holy Spirit was first poured out, people from many different nations and languages were amazed that each one could hear the disciples of Jesus proclaiming the wonders of God in their native languages through the gift of tongues. Some marveled at this miracle, but others responded with ridicule and said, "They have had too much wine." (Acts 2:1–13) Well, this explanation certainly makes sense to me. Who *hasn't* been at a social function where an over-zealous drinker will start spouting off foreign languages and laws of physics and so on?

> *Acts 2:14–21* "*Then Peter stood up with the Eleven, raised his voice and addressed the crowd: "Fellow Jews and all of you who live in Jerusalem, let me explain this to you; listen carefully to what I say. These men are not drunk, as you suppose. It's only nine in the morning! No, this is what was spoken by the prophet Joel: 'In the last days, God says, I will pour out my Spirit on all people. Your sons and daughters will prophesy, your young men will see visions, your old men will dream dreams. Even on my servants, both men and women, I will pour out my Spirit in those days, and they will prophesy. I will show wonders in the heaven above and signs on the earth below, blood and fire and billows of smoke. The sun will be turned to darkness and the moon to blood before the coming of the great and glorious day of the Lord. And everyone who calls on the name of the Lord will be saved.'"*

The way I see it, there are three ways to interpret this Scripture:

1. The "last days" have already happened, and we missed it. I choose not to subscribe to this theory.

2. The "last days" were not during the life of Peter, and so we should expect another outpouring of the Spirit before the official "last days." Or. . . .

3. The "last days" referred to in Acts started with the death and resurrection of Christ, and will continue until the destruction of the world and the return of Christ.

Now, I won't try to convince you which scenario is theologically correct, but my gut feeling is that the end of the world has not yet happened, and the earth has not yet been destroyed. (There are some who might disagree, but that is a topic for another book.)

Since there are so many opinions and positions on this issue, our attitude and approach toward the Holy Spirit and the gifts of the Spirit can only be one of expectant faith.

A Summary of Purpose

I believe the best way of summarizing the purposes of the Holy Spirit—if that were possible—is to examine Scripture on the subject. 1 Corinthians 12:4–10 lists the gifts of the Spirit as being *wisdom, knowledge, faith, healing, miraculous powers, prophecy, distinguishing between spirits, tongues,* and *interpretation of tongues*. I would like to separate these gifts into four groups as a way of explaining the work of the Holy Spirit in our lives.

Gifts of Spiritual Wisdom

Wisdom, Knowledge, and *Prophecy* reveal the mind and ways and purposes of God.

> *1 Corinthians 2:15–16 "The spiritual man makes judgments about all things, but he himself is not subject to any man's judgment: 'For who has known the mind of the Lord that he may instruct him?' But we have the mind of Christ."*

The Spirit *reveals the mind of Christ* and His will, primarily through Scripture and divine revelation. We are called to make judgments about the world around us, judging by the standard of Christ, but we are not to judge others or the condition of their souls. This is very often misunderstood; there is a difference between being spiritually wise and being judgmental. For example, if I were to pass a prostitute on the street, it would be judgmental for me to make an evaluation of the condition of her soul, but it would be wise to assume that there is something missing in her life, and that "something" could very well be the love and salvation of Christ. One view is judgmental; the other is concern resulting from the love of Christ and the knowledge of His resurrection. Now if she were to offer to baby-sit my children, I could ask 'Who am I to judge her?' or I could make a value judgment about the information I have and politely decline.

The Spirit reveals the mind of Christ to us so that we are able to live wisely as Christians, not blindly excusing every type of immorality and sin under the guise of being "non-judgmental."

Gifts of Faith

Those who have the gift of *Faith* are steadfast in the assurance of God's sovereignty and covenants and are unmoved by the wind and waves around them. Some Christians seem to have a supernatural gift of faith, while most others build faith over a period of time. The gift of Faith is impossible without the initial revelation of Christ through the Holy Spirit, but free-will returns the responsibility to us in our response to this revelation. As we choose to believe, the Spirit is able to work *Healing* and *Miracles* in our lives. This process is continuous throughout the Christian life. In Matthew 13:58, it is said of Jesus' hometown, " . . . he did not do many miracles there because of their lack of faith."

Gifts of Worship & Prayer

Another purpose of the Spirit is to help us be true worshipers of the Father.

John 4:23–24 "Yet a time is coming and has now come when the true worshipers will worship the Father in Spirit and truth, for they are the kind of worshipers the Father seeks. God is Spirit, and his worshipers must worship in Spirit and in Truth."

Romans 8:26–27 explains this further:

"In the same way, the Spirit helps us in our weakness. We do not know what we ought to pray for, but the Spirit himself inter-

cedes for us with groans that words cannot express. And He who searches our hearts knows the mind of the Spirit, because the Spirit intercedes for the saints in accordance with God's will."

Essentially, the Spirit helps us worship and pray in a way that is pleasing to the Father. The gifts of *Tongues* and *Interpretation of Tongues* are a part of this process.

Gifts of Spiritual Discernment

Finally, the Spirit helps us in the *Distinguishing of Spirits*. This is the reason a spiritually dead church is vulnerable to false prophets and heretical teachers. I believe this is what Christ was referring to when he said, "Wherever there is a carcass, there the vultures will gather." (Matthew 24:28) Sometimes, with all the "new and improved" theology making its way into the churches, it takes a gift of discernment to distinguish between sound doctrine and heresy.

Now, although I have separated the Spiritual gifts into four categories, some of the gifts could just as easily fit into one of the other categories. For example, the gift of Faith could be a gift of worship, since it requires faith to truly worship God. So the categories are just meant to be helpful guidelines, not hard-and-fast truths.

The Promise

Most importantly, the Holy Spirit *is* the precious gift promised to us by Christ himself and poured out at Pentecost. It is a difficult concept for the world around us to accept, but nevertheless, it is a reality we need to embrace once again if we are to witness the full life in the Spirit He intended for us.

> *John 14:15–18 "If you love me, you will obey what I command. And I will ask the Father and he will give you another Counselor to be with you **forever**—The Spirit of Truth. The world cannot accept Him, because it neither sees Him nor knows Him. But*

you know Him, for He lives with you and will be in you. I will not leave you as orphans; I will come to you." (emphasis added)

In short, Christ promised the gift of His Holy Spirit for the purpose of sustaining the very life we receive at the moment of conversion. This gift was never meant to be tossed aside; it was meant to guide us for the rest of our Christian journey—a gift to be nurtured and embraced. The Holy Spirit is the very presence and wisdom and power of God, and if we wish to see healing in our churches and in our homes and in our society, it will require humbling ourselves and asking the Lord to reintroduce the power of His presence to our congregations.

The Fruit of the Spirit

Galatians 5:22–26 "But the fruit of the Spirit is love, joy, peace, patience, kindness, goodness, faithfulness, gentleness and self-control. Against such things there is no law. Those who belong to Christ Jesus have crucified the sinful nature with its passions and desires. Since we live by the Spirit, let us keep in step with the Spirit. Let us not become conceited, provoking and envying each other."

Bringing all of this together, the spiritual Christian, and consequently the spiritual Church, keeps an attitude of humble obedience and purity, embracing the guidance and the gifts of the Holy Spirit. As a result, we will have "the mind of Christ," producing a great harvest of the spiritual fruit listed in the Scripture above.

Next, we will be taking a brief intermission, and before you say it, I realize books aren't supposed to have intermissions; but as I am writing, I tend to be a little scatter-brained, and I have a difficult time staying on message. So by introducing the concept of book intermissions, it gives me a place to drop these extra writings without having to sneak them into one of the chapters.

In the first part of this book, I've introduced some of the essentials of our Christian faith, but you will notice I have mentioned very little about the fact that we have an enemy who seeks to undermine every one of these truths. Obviously, to truly engage the battle we must first acknowledge the existence of our adversary and learn as much as possible about his strategies. So following the First Intermission, Part II will be devoted to engaging this spiritual battle.

FIRST INTERMISSION
"if only . . ."

Several months prior to writing this book, I was sitting in my car at a fast food restaurant drinking a cup of coffee as part of my waking up ritual. It was a dreary day with the rain beating on the windshield, and I was vainly searching for a reason to be excited about going to work. I remember being particularly irritated about the fact that my coffee cup warned me in no uncertain terms that the coffee would be hot, and it wasn't.

So as I was sitting, staring out the window, I noticed across the parking lot, a daycare center next door, and the front of it resembled a retail toy outlet more than it did a daycare center. I won't give the actual name, but it was something whimsical like "KinderFun" or "Lots-o-Laffs" or "Drop-N-Run"—you get the picture. As I watched the parents stop in front, drop off their little toddlers and then pull away, I remember being deeply saddened by the whole scenario. It caused me to stop and think, "If only they knew the value of those little souls they are entrusting to the care of a stranger."

Please don't misunderstand, my heart really goes out to those women who earnestly desire to stay home and raise their children, but their circumstances require them to work. But I can't help but ask myself how we've gotten to this place as a society where children are viewed as hindrances to career goals, and stay-at-home mothers are treated like second class citizens. At what point in our history did the woman executive start commanding more respect than a mother who is at her wit's end trying to mold and shape the next generation?

snowballs taking chances

    I often wonder how many decisions in life we would make differently if only we knew the eternal outcome.

If only... that frazzled mother could see how precious her sacrifice is to God and to her child, and if only her husband would tell her how much he appreciates her (more than twice a year), maybe she would be less likely to seek affirmation and praise through her work outside of the home.

If only... that mother considering an abortion could touch the face of her child just once...

If only she could tickle the feet of her baby and hear the precious giggles...

If only she had the chance to kiss the wrinkled, pudgy hands of her little boy after he has been playing in the tub too long...

If only for one day she could feel the pain of that couple who so desperately want a son or daughter but are unable to have children...

If only she had the opportunity to meet the men and women whose lives could one day be touched, or even saved, by her child...

If only she knew that the emotional pain from abortion would be far worse than any inconvenience that the baby would cause...

If only someone close to her would care enough to put a loving arm around her to help carry the burden...

If only she could see the tears of Christ as the doctors dispose of the gift he had given her...
Maybe she would not allow her joy to be stolen from her.

if only…

If only… that man considering being unfaithful to his wife could see the end of his life; how wrong he was about the happiness and fulfillment that he would find in infidelity…

If only he could see the broken heart of his wife and how she for years blamed herself and constantly wondered and speculated about how inferior she must have been…

If he could hear the sobs of his children as they lay awake at night wondering, if only they had been better kids, would daddy have stayed?

If only he could see the eternal consequences of breaking a covenant before God…

If only he could see the eternal consequences for his children, who might one day reject the whole existence of God because of his selfishness…

If only he could see how he would spend the rest of his life frantically running, hiding, lying, rationalizing, explaining, blame shifting, and finally collapsing from the weight of sin that never leaves him or allows him to enjoy another day for as long as he lives… Maybe then the stolen pleasures of sin that are chasing him would not overtake him.

If only… we honored our commitments and lived out our faith…

If only we had the sense not to throw away our future for present satisfaction…

If only we saw others as God sees them, created in his image…

If only we as a nation devoted as much time to God and family as we do to entertainment...

If only we defended our faith as vigorously as others defend their right to depravity and self-degradation...

If only any of this were actually possible... Only if... we put our hope and faith in the Creator, our God, and live our lives sold-out for him, relying on his strength and forgiveness; only then will he turn and show us favor and heal our families and our land.

PART II
engaging the battle

CHAPTER 7
the devil in the details

"For our struggle is not against flesh and blood . . ."

World Class Denial

In chapter four, I mentioned the importance of accepting all of Scripture as the inspired Word of God. Unfortunately, with that responsibility comes the realization that we have an enemy who seeks our demise. As Christians, it is easy to become overly casual when it comes to issues of sin and Satan. More often than not, we avoid at all costs any mention of Satan and his demons because it gives us an uneasy feeling, and worse than that, it gives rise to questions about heaven, hell, and eternity, which we are not equipped to answer. So what is our approach to these issues? It is world-class denial. It is the ill-conceived hope that if we don't acknowledge the "dark side," it will cease to exist, and then, maybe if we rationalize enough, we can transform the verses of Scripture dealing with Satan into metaphors.

I think it would be interesting to take some verses and revise them to fit into this version of "denial-based" theology: Mark 5:6–13 (revised)

When he saw Jesus from a distance, he ran and fell on his knees in front of him. He shouted at the top of his voice, "What do you want with me, Jesus, Son of the Most High God? Swear to God that you won't torture me!" For Jesus had said to him, "Come out of this man you metaphor representing a severe anger problem!" Then Jesus asked him, "What is your name?" "My name is Metaphorico's Legion," he replied, "for we are many." And he begged Jesus again and again not to send them out of the area. A large herd of pigs, known for their willingness as metaphorical hosts, was feeding on the nearby hillside. Metaphorico begged Jesus, "Send us among the pigs; allow us to go into them." He gave them permission, and the legion of metaphors came out and went into the pigs. The herd, about two thousand in number, rushed down the steep bank into the lake and were drowned, metaphorically speaking.

As you can see, any Bible-believing Christian of reasonably sound mind will have a very difficult time rationalizing away the existence of Satan and demons. The Bible is clear that Satan is a very real, tangible, spiritual being who needs to be reckoned with on a daily basis, and we need to be wiser in our dealing with the enemy.

The Guy in Red Tights

If it seems I am being rather flippant in my approach to the existence of Satan, it is for the sole purpose of underscoring the need to acknowledge this threat to our eternal reward. In much the same way, our approach to Satan has an air of flippancy about it. Somewhere in the back of our minds, we see Satan as this cartoon character in red tights with a pitchfork. We give him a little wink as we get as close as we can to sin without getting burned—much like "snowballs taking chances," not realizing that each time we flirt with sin, a little of the life of Christ in us is melted away. If we could get one glimpse of the nature of Satan, we would not be winking at him, nor would we be naming vacuum cleaners or sports teams after him.

In many ways our approach to Satan resembles my experiences in army basic training. In an effort to train for a real enemy, we would have these training missions during which we would hide out for long periods of time in the middle of the night, freezing to death, waiting for an imaginary enemy with imaginary bullets to attack us in our imaginary bunkers. Even though we took the training seriously and tried to stay awake, there was no way to manufacture the sense of urgency and desperation that we would feel if the enemy was real and using live ammunition. In much the same way, our tendency as Christians is to look and to act as if we are preparing for a real adversary, but the sense of urgency is missing. Not until a real spiritual bullet has grazed us do we realize that the battle is real, and many times our reaction is something like, "Hey! No Fair! He's shooting real bullets!" But as formidable as our adversary may be, it is the impending judgment of God that should strike in us the greatest fear.

> *Matthew 10:28 "Do not be afraid of those who kill the body but cannot kill the soul. Rather be afraid of the one who can destroy both soul and body in hell."*
> *- Jesus*

Very much is at stake; our adversary is real. Fight valiantly, because your soul and the souls of those who are watching your example may be at stake. "In your struggle against sin, you have not yet resisted to the point of shedding your blood." (Heb. 12:14) The "fleeting pleasures" of sin may seem so enticing at the moment, but eternally speaking, they have the power to put you on a spiritual course resulting in the rejection of your Christian faith. Eternity in hell is a high price to pay for momentary pleasure.

Satan's Ally

> *John 2:24–25* The Sin Nature

> *But Jesus would not entrust himself to them (his followers), for He knew all men. He did not need man's testimony about man, **for he knew what was in a man.** (emphasis added)*

Did you ever stop to think about why you never hear someone talk about falling into a good habit? I have never heard anyone say, "You know, I just can't help it; every chance I get I keep helping people and giving away money to the poor. Why, just the other day I found myself wanting to shovel the sidewalk of my neighbor who hates me. God bless the fellow." Now, this is not to say that people don't do charitable things, but it takes an effort, and sometimes it is even for selfish reasons, like wanting to be seen in a favorable light. Sin, on the other hand, takes no effort at all. We are drawn to sin naturally, and to live a righteous life of integrity takes work. This is the meaning of the passage above, when it states that Jesus "knew what was in a man." Our sin nature, sometimes called the "flesh," is concerned only with self-fulfillment, and it acts as an ally to Satan.

Free-will

Our sin nature only starts to make sense when you look at it from a free-will standpoint. Right from the start, God gave man the right to make his own decisions, and I might add, the right to suffer the consequences of those decisions. No other creature on earth was given this right. When was the last time you saw a spider getting creative and building a nest out of straw? When have you ever seen a robin abandoning its eggs to go live with another robin? These things just don't happen. Our Creator has programmed into the brains of all other creatures the decisions they are to make, and they obey because they are obligated to. If I hold a gun to your head and say, "Tell me you like the way I write," it will probably mean a lot less to me than if you voluntarily say, "I like the way you write; you should get your book published." The free-will of humanity allows God to be glorified—or saddened—by our decisions.

But, as is often the case, upon the creation of Adam and Eve, their sin nature wanted what it could not have; hence the fall of mankind. Free-will is what makes the salvation of mankind glorifying to God because he does not force us to love or to choose him. So in a sense, the very thing God put in place to give validity to the worship of him—namely free choice—Satan uses in conjunction with the flesh to plan our downfall. This all seems a little ridiculous until one takes an honest look at his life to find that this is exactly the way it happens. The Apostle Paul writes about his epic struggle with the sin nature in his letter to the Romans (Keep in mind, this is the same Apostle Paul who wrote many of the books of the New Testament):

Romans 7:14–25 "We know that the law is spiritual; but I am unspiritual, sold as a slave to sin. I do not understand what I do. For what I want to do I do not do, but what I hate I do. And if I do what I do not want to do, I agree that the law is good. As it is, it is no longer I myself who do it, but it is sin living in me. I know that nothing good lives in me, that is, in my sinful nature. For I have the desire to do what is good, but I cannot carry it out. For what I do is not the good I want to do; no, the evil I do not want to do—this I keep on doing. Now if I do what I do not want to do, it is no longer I who do it, but it is sin living in me that does it."

"So I find this law at work: When I want to do good, evil is right there with me. For in my inner being I delight in God's law; but I see another law at work in the members of my body waging war against the law of my mind and making me a prisoner of the law of sin at work within my members. What a wretched man I am! Who will rescue me from this body of death? Thanks be to God—through Jesus Christ our Lord!"

Now the first time you read through this account by the Apostle Paul, you might scratch your head and wonder, "What in the heck did I just read? Did he say, 'I did not do what I wish I had done, had I already done the doable thing I thought I would have done, had I done did it?' Was that a quote from Edgar Allan Poe, or Sigmund Freud, or someone else who had lost their mind?" But the beauty of the way it is written is that it shows how maddening the struggle against the sin nature can be. It also gives us a rare glimpse into the spiritual battles of one of the most inspired and godly men of the Bible. Our tendency is to characterize the saints of Scripture as men and women who floated around anointing people and doing miracles and striking poses. The reality is, they lived difficult and sometimes tortured lives, and they fought very real battles with sin, sickness, rejection and martyrdom. It is common to think we are the only ones who struggle with such base and sinful tendencies, so this passage by Paul comes as quite a relief. But thanks be to God, he has rescued us from this "body of death . . . through Jesus Christ our Lord."

The Nature of the Beast

> *1 Peter 5:8–9 "Be self-controlled and alert. Your enemy the devil prowls around like a roaring lion looking for someone to devour.* **Resist him, standing firm in the faith,** *because you know that your brothers throughout the world are undergoing the same kind of sufferings." (emphasis added)*

For whatever reason, it seems as if the devil is rarely spoken of from the pulpit. I don't know if it is the pastor's fear of being labeled as one who is a few candles shy of a vigil or as the guy who sits on his rooftop with a tinfoil hat waiting for a signal from outer space. Or it might just be the hate-mail he receives when he ventures outside the topic of God's love. But whatever the reason, our adversary is real and needs to be acknowledged. Don't misunderstand; I am not advocating looking for Satan under every rock or blaming him for every time you have a bad day or you can't find your car keys. But the vivid imagery in the Scripture above makes it obvious that we are to be more alert to his schemes than we usually are.

The question becomes, in real world terms, what did Peter mean when he said, "Your enemy the devil prowls around like a roaring lion looking for someone to devour"? What it means to me as a husband and father is that Satan will do everything in his power to destroy my marriage and family, minimizing the eternal effect I am able to have as a Christian man on my family and on the world around me.

Satan is exceptionally patient when it comes to seeking our demise. He is willing to take small victories, like allowing an argument with a man and his wife to smolder for a while. Then the smoldering turns

the devil in the details

to resentment as the husband thinks, "I can't believe how she showed a complete lack of concern or respect when she accused me of that. I think I even noticed a smirk of victory as she brought up everything I have ever done wrong in the history of our marriage. And how she accused *me* of being selfish! I'll show her selfish; I can't believe I even bother trying to keep my thoughts pure for her; after all, I am a man. I've got needs just like any other man. I'm not going to be the one to give in and apologize this time. When was the last time *she* apologized first? I should have listened to my friends; we never should have gotten married in the first place."

In a separate room his wife is thinking, "I've never seen such hate in his eyes. Our whole marriage has been one betrayal after another. When was the last time I've seen any affection that didn't come with strings attached? I'll bet he thinks I don't notice how much time he spends on the computer late at night. So much for the fairytale romance. Is this what we've been reduced to? Existing in the same house together, sitting in front of the television for three hours each night, never talking, never resolving any of our problems. Is this what I signed up for? Is this really what God intended for marriage? Maybe it was a mistake from the start. Maybe I wasn't listening and missed God's best for me. After all, wouldn't God want me to be happy? If I could get half as much attention from him as I get from the guys at the office, I wouldn't be so miserable. But if it takes a harmless conversation over lunch with a coworker to get my needs met, then so be it. If he only knew how many proposals I turn down each week, he'd start showing me a little attention. I should have listened to my parents and held out for a better man."

Can you sense the devil starting to prowl in this scenario, maybe circling and licking his chops a little? Then, if he can get us to start resenting God for whatever difficulties life presents, he is not far from a meal. Unfortunately, too often we set the table for him because of our lack of awareness to his tactics or even to his existence.

The Antidote to Complacency

If we ever start to become complacent and forget that Satan is prowling—say for example the rare instance when life is ho-humming along and no major problems or decisions are on the horizon—all we need to do is read the daily newspaper to remind us of his existence. Then we should ask ourselves these questions: If human beings are basically good at heart (as popular culture would contend), and Satan is not a real living spiritual being, what is it that would cause a man to detonate a bomb strapped to himself, scattering body parts all over a crowded market? What is it that would cause a mother to drown her very own children, or a father—who should be the protector of his family—to violate his own daughter? What is it that would cause a set of parents to chain a child to a mattress and to abuse and starve the child to death? How is it that an entire society can be convinced that it is acceptable to enslave or exterminate a whole race of fellow human beings? How is it that a whole society can be convinced that the murdering of unborn children is an acceptable practice? How is it that men, women and little children can be exploited and abused for the purposes of entertainment, and how is it that a market exists for such depravity?

And finally, why did the Son of God allow a society (of basically good people) to torture him, beat him, spit on him and crucify him, if it weren't to save us from this wretched condition in which we find ourselves? Was it to conquer an enemy that does not exist?

Romans 16:19–20 ". . . I want you to be wise about what is good, and innocent about what is evil. The God of peace will soon crush Satan under your feet."

Since the beginning of time, God's people have fallen prey to misconceptions about the existence of Satan and his tactics. As Christians, we need to take a closer look at how the enemy has disguised himself and cleverly established areas of sin and depraved philosophy within the Church. But to do this, we must first examine how "truth" has gradually vanished from our culture.

CHAPTER 8
muddy waters

Buckling the Belt of Truth

*Jer. 7:28 "Therefore say to them, 'This is the nation that has not obeyed the Lord its God or responded to correction. **Truth has perished; it has vanished from their lips.**'" (emphasis added)*

What is Truth?

One of the most fascinating questions of all time, and one that our society asks with increasing frequency, was asked of Jesus as He was being questioned by Pilate before the crucifixion. First, Pilate asks Jesus if He is a king, and Jesus answers,

John 18:37 "You are right in saying I am a king. In fact, for this reason I was born, and for this I came into the world, to testify to the truth. Everyone on the side of the truth listens to me."

To which Pilate asks, "What is truth?" (v. 38)

At first glance, this question doesn't seem too profound, but when it is taken within the context of the glory of Rome, it speaks volumes. Much like America, Rome had achieved tremendous wealth and unequaled prominence, and to be considered a citizen of Rome was the ultimate honor. Because of their reputation, the Romans weren't immediately threatened militarily, so they had lots of time on their hands to sit around, debating the meaning of life and the definition of truth. Much like the intellectually elite in America, the Romans believed that the brilliance was in *the asking of the question*, not in the seeking of an answer. After all, to seek an answer would just show how closed-minded you were. Pilate didn't wait around for an answer because he had already proven to Jesus how wise he was, just by asking the question.

Only the Christians deal in absolutes.

To the "enlightened" class, truth is relative; in other words, there are no absolutes. One of the most telling lines in movie history was uttered with great "wisdom" by Obi-Wan Kenobi in the final Star Wars film, "Revenge of the Sith." (Actually, there may be another pre-post-sequel in production, but I'll assume this was the third and final episode out of six or nine; but who's counting?) The line was delivered in response to Anakin's comment, "You are either with me, or my enemy." With great moral clarity and *absolute* resolve, Obi-Wan replies, "Only a Sith deals in absolutes."

Surely this contradiction has been beaten into the ground, but it is too comical to pass up. So I'll ask the question: How can you be so absolute that there are no absolutes? The not-so-veiled comment by Obi-Wan was obviously making the point that those who believe in absolutes or claim to follow moral absolutes belong to the dark side. If there was ever any doubt about the entertainment industry's agenda, Obi-Wan's comment should help clear it up.

Darth Christ?

According to George Lucas, Jesus Christ would have been the darkest Sith Lord ever to live because no one spoke with more absolute moral clarity than He did. Here is one example:

*John 14:6 I am the way, **the truth**, and the life. No one comes to the Father except through me" (emphasis added)*

Not only did Jesus speak about truth; He claimed to *be* the truth. One would think that if Christ is the Truth, the teachings of His Church would be steadfastly rooted in Scripture. The problem is, as society deteriorates, the philosophies of that society seep into the fabric of the Church, and the lines between truth and falsehood become blurred.

The First United Church of the Guilt-free Pleasures

To find a tangible example of how this deterioration has affected the present-day church, I needed to look no further than my local paper. There was a story about an excommunicated priest who started a "breakaway congregation," which was set up to appeal to all of those who have "ever felt burned by the church's absolutism." The ex-priest goes on to explain, "Anyone who professes absolute authority or absolute knowledge, as the church does, can lead people into tragedy."

The Christian Church was founded on the absolute truths and teachings of Christ—I should say on Christ himself. If there are no absolutes—for example, the existence of heaven or hell or the afterlife—going to church is one of the most intellectually bankrupt ideas known to mankind.

> *1 Corinthians 15:32 "If the dead are not raised, let us eat and drink, for tomorrow we die."*

The greatest contradiction about this breakaway "church" is its name; I won't give the full name, but I will mention that it includes the name of Christ. Yet at the same time, the ex-priest doesn't believe in "asserting the deity of Jesus Christ." That is like saying, "Everybody gather 'round. We're going to start a church founded on a very important guy who claimed to be God but really wasn't. Other than that, he was really wise and had enough neat sayings to keep us busy for a while. As a matter of fact, we won't mention any of the mean ones if they make you feel uncomfortable."

The most tragic part of the story is, at last check, he had approximately 800 followers—and every one of them will spend eternity in hell if they reject the deity of Christ. It is a hard truth to swallow, but according to Scripture, it is absolute.

Is Christ helpless?

Now I could play the progressive's advocate and ask, "Isn't Christ powerful enough to maintain His standard of Truth within His own Church?" As I said in chapter six, obedience to Christ is one crucial element to seeing the power and blessing of the Holy Spirit within a particular church. So if the members of that church begin lowering their standards of behavior in regard to sin, the Spirit of Christ—or the Spirit of Truth—is withdrawn, and chaos ensues. I will quote again the passage from John making this point:

John 14:15–18 "If you love me, you will obey what I command. And I will ask the Father and he will give you another Counselor to be with you forever—The Spirit of Truth. The world cannot accept him, because it neither sees him nor knows him.

"The world cannot accept him . . ." It is pointless for us, as Christians, to sit around and whine that the secular world and the entertainment industry are undermining the Truth; it's their *job*—it's what they do. They don't have the ability to accept the Spirit of Truth. This is not a new or enlightened concept at all; from the beginning of time, as a society becomes more secular or Godless, the Truth is one of the first things to get discarded. The next step in the dismantling of the Church is the act of redefining sin.

Redefining Sin

A good sign that it is time to head for higher ground is when members of the Body of Christ—members of any Christian denomination—begin endorsing sinful patterns of behavior, and even ordaining those who openly practice them. To conquer the sin in our lives—and consequently, in the church—there must be a common understanding of exactly what defines sin. This is made more difficult when some church leaders muddy the waters by establishing gray areas of sin. So in order to establish a biblical definition, I'd like to go to the book of Genesis to study the fall of mankind.

A Sinful Piece of Fruit?

Many people view the story of Adam and Eve to be a rather simplistic explanation for the fall of humanity, and others might see it as God using a metaphor for some other more serious type of sin. But since it is in Scripture, I would like to believe it has profound significance just as it is. By choosing the forbidden fruit as the first temptation of man, God takes an object, which in all other situations would be considered good, and makes it off-limits to Adam and Eve. The object itself was not inherently evil, but by God's decision to limit Adam and Eve's actions in relation to the fruit, sin becomes possible. By doing this, He is setting the standard for the definition of sin for the rest of time and eternity.

> *The definition of sin is this: Sin is simply disobeying God or His established commandments, on any particular, whether in thought or in action.*

Adam and Eve had one command: Don't touch the fruit. And that was all it took to begin the downward spiral of humanity.

But it doesn't feel wrong . . .

As modern Christians, a difficult concept to accept is that God gets to decide what sin is and what it is not. It doesn't seem fair. After all, "God made me this way, *He* gave me these desires and tendencies; *He* put this particular circumstance in my life or at least allowed it." Again, there was nothing inherently evil about the fruit, but it was assigned a particular spiritual significance by God and was made off-limits to Adam and Eve. This is the magnificence of God's creation; He creates us with intrinsically good desires and emotions and personalities and talents, and then He says, "Of all of these wondrous things you may partake, but only within these confines." Now this might seem rather sadistic of God until you examine the lives of those who throw off all inhibition and engage in every desire that comes to mind. What you will witness will be the utter pain, humiliation, disease, addiction, heartache, and isolation that this approach has to offer—yet we still demand our right to all of it.

Without limitations, we would very quickly descend to the lowest point imaginable. A while back, I was at the zoo with my family, and as we were walking we noticed a bunch of kids pointing at something and laughing. As you can imagine, we became curious and walked over to see what the fuss was all about. It turns out the king and queen of the jungle were working on making a prince, and it occurred to me, as a society, we're not too far from resembling the animal kingdom, especially in the entertainment we choose.

Nevertheless, before we stray too far from the Adam and Eve example, the question becomes, why didn't God just put the tree out of reach or in another garden? Why tempt Adam and Eve in the first place? Why make something so beautiful and desirable if you aren't going to let us enjoy it? Because right from the start our Creator intended for us to exercise free-will. Two things about the fruit made it irresistible; first, its appearance, and second, the fact that it was off-limits. It is the time-tested story of humanity—we want what we cannot have, and we desire to do what we are told not to do.

When I was in high school I worked at a produce store, and it was my job at the end of the day to mop the floors to prepare for business the next day. In my exuberance to do a thorough job—and maybe partly because I had heard you weren't supposed to—I decided to mix two undisclosed cleaning products to create a secret cleaning solution. To my delight, it started to hiss and smoke, and I proceeded to mop the floors, but after acquiring a headache, I decided to switch to a more traditional cleaning product. Because of my natural desire to do what I knew I should not, several people went home with headaches that day, but fortunately no one died.

Who Muddied the Waters?

So back to the original question, how did we get to the place, as God's Church, of debating whether or not we should "update" our definition of sin? Now, if we had not been given the Scriptures to help us identify sin, this confusion among the shepherds of the Church might almost make sense.

> *Romans 7:7 "Indeed I would not have known what sin was except through the law."*

But the reality is, sin has been clearly defined by the Word of God, and there no longer remains any excuse, but only the fearful prospect of judgment.

> *Hebrews 10:26–27 "If we deliberately keep on sinning after we have received the knowledge of the truth, no sacrifice for sins is left, but only a fearful expectation of judgment and of raging fire that will consume the enemies of God."*

Those who seek to undermine the holiness and purity of the Bride of Christ, the Church, are identified by the passage above as "enemies of God." This sounds a bit harsh, but Christ himself called the Scribes and Pharisees "hypocrites," "blind guides" and a "brood of vipers." Church leaders are doing no favors for those trapped in habitual sin by coddling them or ordaining them or shuffling them from church to church. On the contrary, they could very well be contributing to their eternal damnation, not to mention the devastating, long-term repercussions for the laity.

> *1 Corinthians 6:9–10 "Do you not know that the wicked will not inherit the kingdom of God? Do not be deceived: Neither the sexually immoral nor idolaters nor adulterers nor male prostitutes nor homosexual offenders nor thieves nor the greedy nor drunkards nor slanderers nor swindlers will inherit the kingdom of God."*

This verse is not intended to be an exhaustive list of all the sins of damnation. In order to understand it fully, I believe it is crucial to distinguish between those who struggle with serious sin and those who proudly identify themselves with it. For example, if you actively participate in parades celebrating any of these things, or if you are involved in lobbying church leadership to be more "progressive" by sanctioning them, or if you just simply identify with a particular sinful lifestyle and have no intention or desire to change—you are in grave danger of bringing eternal disaster upon yourself.

> *Isaiah 3:9 "The look on their faces testifies against them; they parade their sin like Sodom; they do not hide it. Woe to them! They have brought disaster upon themselves."*

On the other hand, upon examination of the list of sins from 1 Corinthians, the vast majority of us would be in a whole lot of eternal trouble if the passage stopped right there. After all, most of us have been guilty of at least one or more of these sins at some point in our lives. Thankfully, it continues:

> *1 Corinthians 6:11 "And that is what some of you were. But you were washed, you were sanctified, you were justified in the name of the Lord Jesus Christ and by the Spirit of our God."*

This verse offers our first clue regarding where we should start in our struggle against sin, which we will cover in the next chapter. But first, I think it would be prudent to examine the strategy Satan used to infiltrate the ranks of the army of God. For a step by step account, we need to look no further than the book of Romans. The study of human history should keep us from making the same mistakes over and over again, but sadly, we stubbornly demand our right to make these mistakes, and we pay the price.

Doing as the Romans Did

> *Romans 1:20–25 For since the creation of the world God's invisible qualities—his eternal power and divine nature—have been clearly seen, being understood from what has been made, so that men are without excuse. **For although they knew God, they neither glorified him as God nor gave thanks***

to him, but their thinking became futile *and their foolish hearts were darkened. Although they claimed to be wise, they became fools and exchanged the glory of the immortal God for images made to look like mortal man and birds and animals and reptiles.*
Therefore God gave them over in the sinful desires of their hearts to sexual impurity for the degrading of their bodies with one another. **They exchanged the truth of God for a lie, and worshipped and served created things rather than the Creator**—*who is forever praised. Amen.*
Because of this, God gave them over to shameful lusts. *Even their women exchanged natural relations for unnatural ones. In the same way the men also abandoned natural relations with women and were inflamed with lust for one another. Men committed indecent acts with other men, and received in themselves the due penalty for their perversion.* (emphasis added)

This pattern, which the Apostle Paul clearly outlines in his letter to the Romans, has been followed almost to the letter by our nation.

First: Our nation was founded on the Judeo-Christian system of beliefs by those who were seeking religious freedom.

Second: We decided, once we were prosperous, that God was no longer worth acknowledging, and we took Him out of our schools and now out of our courthouses. Our thinking became "futile."

Hosea 13:6 "When I fed them, they were satisfied; when they were satisfied, they became proud; then they forgot me."

Third: Truth is sacrificed. "They exchanged the truth of God for a lie . . ."

Fourth: Our *"foolish hearts became darkened,"* and we began worshiping created things instead of the Creator (Mother Earth, stars, trees, animals, Hollywood, etc.)

Fifth: The natural, pure gift of sexuality became confused and distorted.

Sixth: (Our own unique step) Members of God's Church decide that God has changed His mind about certain types of sin and attempt to normalize it within the Church.

The Birth of Moral Relativism

One thing in particular that stands out to me is that when we reject God by refusing to acknowledge Him in the public square, He allows us to destroy ourselves with our own sinful nature and desires. Right and wrong cease to be as clear as they once were, and we begin creating our own moral standard.

Judges 17:16 "Each man did what was right in his own eyes."

Right and wrong have now become relative to society's whims, and as society deteriorates, right and wrong drift closer and closer together and at some point, switch places.

Isaiah 5:20 Woe to those who call evil good and good evil, who put darkness for light and light for darkness, who put bitter for sweet and sweet for bitter.

This trading of places of good and evil is never a quick process; as a matter of fact, it could take decades or even centuries. But because of our sin nature, the progression is always toward evil rather than righteousness.

The Key to Boiling Frogs

I've always considered the analogy of the "boiling pot of frogs" to be quite appropriate when explaining the evil-for-good transition. It is overused, but it represents a prominent strategy of Satan, so it bears repeating. The idea is—and don't ask me who discovered this fact—if you were to throw frogs into a pot of boiling water, they would quickly jump out. But if you were to place the frogs in a pot of cool water and slowly increase the heat, the frogs would not try to escape, but they would allow themselves to be boiled to death. (I have not tried this at home, so please don't report me to PETA.)

The entertainment industry is famous for perfecting the art of boiling Christian frogs. I remember the outrage several years ago when "NYPD Blue" debuted on ABC. There were protests and boycotts and letters written, and many of us vowed to never watch the ABC network again. Now, "NYPD Blue" is tame in comparison to many of the shows in primetime, and it has become difficult to decide whom to boycott. The networks now compete to see who can appeal to the lowest life form possible. I've actually heard that they will test their shows in a laboratory by scraping some scum from the inside of a toilet bowl and then testing to see if it multiplies in a Petri dish after exposing it to the new shows.

Because of the advance of technology and the decline of American/Christian standards, the entertainment battle has been steadily losing ground; so instead, we need to focus our energies and resources on transforming the heart of the Christian. As we approach the boiling point, I wonder what it will take to get the average Christian to jump out of the pot. Unfortunately, it usually takes a great disaster to jolt a society back toward reverence to God.

> *Hosea 5:15 "Then I will go back to my place until they admit their guilt. And they will seek my face; in their misery they will earnestly seek me." - God*

Stick a Fork in It

A sure sign that we are quickly becoming hard-boiled frogs is the newfound "tolerance" of serious sin within the Church that I mentioned at the beginning of this chapter. It is like watching a turkey cook on Thanksgiving, waiting for the little red thermometer to pop out—only with a far less desirable outcome. Some Christian denominations are further along in this process than others, but our society on the whole seems to be clamoring for the Church to "get with the program and stop being so . . . so . . . religious and intolerant." As Jesus was instructing his disciples on what signs to look for signaling the "End of the Age," or the end of the world, first he said that the Gospel would be preached in the whole world, and then he warned them,

> *Matthew 24:15–16 "So when you see standing in the holy place 'the abomination that causes desolation,' spoken of through the prophet Daniel—let the reader understand—then let those who are in Judea flee to the mountains."*

I won't even hazard a guess at what *the* "abomination that causes desolation" is. After all, not even the little "cheat" sections of my study Bible are willing to go that far. But I will say that a few of the primary sins that now plague the Church are listed as "abominations" by Scripture, and desolation is the inevitable consequence of those sins. So the trend is certainly toward establishing abominations within the Church.

Friendly Fire

As an example of this softening stance toward sin, I was speaking with the pastor of a church who was explaining to me a dilemma he was facing as he was asked to counsel couples from his church. He said that it was not unusual to have an unmarried couple come to him for counseling on marriage-type issues, and it never occurs to them that the whole approach to their relationship is wrong. Many times, when he would try to raise issues of morality, the parents of those being counseled would become outraged and accuse him of being judgmental. Essentially, he was being asked to endorse the relationship and the living arrangement, and "Oh yeah, can you help us fix our problems without mentioning any of that icky sin and guilt stuff?"

Now, I could have used a different example of sin—maybe one that a larger percentage of the population would find repulsive and destructive to the church—but this is exactly the point. Why have we Christians become so comfortable normalizing *any* type of sin?

Before you plan a book-burning party, let me explain. Not too many years ago I suffered through a quarter-life crisis, sometimes called the "stupidity phase." It is the time period in your life when you suddenly realize that nobody around you seems to recognize how extremely bright and talented you really are. Not only that, the authority figures in your life seem to think that you are incapable of setting your own limits on speed and behavior. It is a time when everyone owes you a life, and nobody is paying up. So you do what any sensible quarter-lifer would do, and you get them back by engaging in every type of self-destructive behavior you can think of.

During *my* stupidity phase, my life was filled with things you'll hear nothing about in this book because my credibility would be shot. But when I look back, I ask myself these questions: Would I have wanted the Church to watch my behavior and say, "Uh-oh. It looks like Tedesco is at it again. Looks like we'll need to revise the definition of sin once more so he doesn't feel guilty on Sunday if he decides to stop in"? Or would I have wanted my parents to say, "We better be careful what we say to him. He is in a very delicate stage, and we don't want to put him over the edge"?

I will not serve a God who is subject to the whims and fancies of the people he created. Also, if we as the Body of Christ do not allow the pastors to pastor—if they have merely become administrators or dispensers of sacraments—can we really expect an outpouring of the Holy Spirit? If the life of the average Christian looks no different than the non-Christian, can we honestly hold out a hand to those who are drowning?

Raging Waters

One of the most emotionally draining events of my life happened one day while hiking with my family in the woods near a raging stream. After walking for a little while, we decided to take a break by standing on the large rocks next to the water, and for just a few seconds we took our eyes off our youngest son Samuel. As life would have it, in those few seconds he strolled over to the edge to rinse his feet and slipped, managing to grab onto the edge of a boulder as he fell. Our eldest son Joshua quickly got our attention, and as I turned, I saw my son, petrified, sliding down the edge of the rock. It was like a bad slow motion scene from a movie, and I have since replayed the scene countless times in my mind. I dove onto the rock, catching the collar of his jacket with no time to spare, and I pulled him to safety. A fraction of a second later and he would have been swept downstream with the whitewater rapids, and by instinct I would have jumped in after him. At that point, my wife would have had to save us both, since my swimming skills have not been finely honed—she would say they are non-existent.

I learned many things that day, not the least of which was there was a reason for the sign that read, "For Your Safety, Please Stay On the Path!" But for the purposes of this chapter, the most relevant lesson would be that in order to help save someone, you must first be on solid rock yourself.

> *Psalm 62:6–7 He alone is my rock and my salvation; he is my fortress, I will not be shaken. My salvation and my honor depend on God; He is my mighty rock, my refuge.*

I believe that sin within the Church causes us to resemble a stream full of people flailing around, hoping to be saved by just a few people on solid footing. If those who are supposed to be helping save others jump off the rock and get sucked under by the current of sin, who is left to help rescue the others? In many ways, because of the slow desensitization of the Church toward sin, we might actually resemble people relaxing on rafts in a calm stream, sipping iced tea and drifting toward the falls. We can see the ripples up ahead, but we are enjoying the ride too much to change course. And, I might add, we get angry with anyone who chooses to warn us—or our kids—about the falls.

Averting Disaster

Romans 8:31 asks, "If God is for us, who can be against us?" By studying the decline of morality within the Church and the resulting effect on our nation, we have seen what happens if God is "*against* us." But how can we shift this trend, as the Church and as individual Christians, toward ensuring that "God is *for* us"? With this question, we engage the battle.

CHAPTER 9
the four keys

"If God is for us..."

2 Chronicles 7:14 "... if my people, who are called by my name, will humble themselves and pray and seek my face and turn from their wicked ways, then I will hear from heaven and will forgive their sin and will heal their land."

God's Promise

In chapter two, I briefly mentioned the Scripture above, but now I would like to examine it more closely, because it contains the four keys necessary to make certain that "God is for us." To understand the setting, Solomon was dedicating the temple he had just finished building for the Lord, and the words of this Scripture passage were part of a covenant God was making with His people as He consecrated the temple. Verse 7:13 helps put it into context:

2 Chronicles 7:13 "When I shut up the heavens so that there is no rain, or command locusts to devour the land or send a plague among my people..."

In other words, God is saying that when Israel sins as a nation and is disciplined by Him, He would establish a way for the Israelites to come back to Him and receive His grace. If He was speaking directly to America, He might have said something like,

"When your country is ravaged by divorce and broken homes, and when your children begin killing each other and are afraid to go to school because you would not let them mention my Name, and when addiction and disease have torn apart your families, and when sin infiltrates my holy Church..."

God has established a way back for us, and we need to take it... soon.

The First Key—Called by His Name

The first key is woven into the phrase, "if my people, who are called by my name." This key is crucial to unlocking the other three because it shows us that God places the responsibility for spiritual revival and the healing of our land squarely on the shoulders of those called by his name. You'll notice he doesn't place the blame for societal deterioration on the un-churched or the un-saved.

The Prodigal Stranger

In the parable of *The Prodigal Son*, the son leaves home with his inheritance and spends it on women and wine before realizing (after spending himself into the poor house) that it wasn't so bad at home where all of his needs were met. After rehearsing his apology, he returned home, expecting the worst. To his amazement, when his father recognized him from afar, he ran to him and hugged him and told his servants to prepare a great feast for his son, who had finally returned home.

Now if after the son had returned home, another guy who had witnessed the whole thing from the road decided, "Hey! I like the way that went! I'm going to give it a try," don't you think the results would have been a bit different? Imagine the scene. The stranger runs across the field (in slow motion, with his hands brushing against the golden wheat) and he prepares to leap into the man's arms, but he is quickly apprehended by the man's servants. Imagine his disappointment as he heard (in slow motion), "Call... security! There... is... some... lunatic... running... across... my... field!"

The first key to this parable—and to the question, "Is God for us?"—is that the prodigal son was exactly *that*—a son, not a stranger. He had the right, as a son, to at least approach the father. For us to be considered sons and daughters, we must first accept the only way provided by the Father to be considered children of God:

Ephesians 1:5–6 In love he predestined us to be adopted as his sons through Jesus Christ, in accordance with his pleasure and will—to the praise of his glorious grace, which he has freely given us in the One he loves.

"God is for us" if and only if we have accepted the death of Christ as payment for our sins. This is the one foundational truth on which the success of our battle against Satan rests. All the striving and therapy and accountability groups and self-help books are futile temporary fixes without the realization that the ultimate final battle has been won in Christ.

Luke 6:47–48 "I will show you what he is like who comes to me and hears my words and puts them into practice. He is like a man building a house, who dug down deep and laid the foundation on rock. When a flood came, a torrent stuck that house but could not shake it, because it was well built."

1 Corinthians 3:11 For no one can lay any foundation other than the one already laid, which is Jesus Christ.

In the account of Joshua and the battle of Jericho, Joshua was preparing for war when he noticed a man standing in front of him with his sword drawn. So he asked him,

"Are you for us or for our enemies?" "Neither," he replied, "but as commander of the army of the Lord I have now come." Then Joshua fell facedown to the ground in reverence, and asked him, "What message does my Lord have for his servant?"

The commander of the Lord's army replied, "Take off your sandals, for the place where you are standing is holy." And Joshua did so. (Joshua 5:13–15)

The commander's message to Joshua was that he needed to acknowledge he was standing on holy ground. Once each of us comes to the awesome realization that it is God the Father who goes into battle before us, we will fall to our knees in reverence, abject humility and repentance, which leads us to the second key.

The Second Key–Humility & Repentance

" . . . if my people . . . will humble themselves . . ."

Returning to the story of the prodigal son, before the son could truly receive and appreciate the grace of the father, he needed to be brought to the place of utter ruin. He had spent all of his money and had been reduced to coveting the scraps of grain he was feeding to the pigs. More often than not, it takes some type of poverty to get us to a place of repentance; it could be financial poverty, relational, physical, emotional, etc. (Every once in a long while, *blessing* from God will lead to thanksgiving and humility, but this is atypical.) Genuine repentance is the key to the Father's grace, which in turn makes all other efforts on our part fruitful. The importance of repentance in restoring our relationship to God cannot be overstated.

Proverbs 28:13 He who conceals his sins does not prosper, but whoever confesses and renounces them finds mercy.

2 Corinthians 7:10 "Godly sorrow brings repentance that leads to salvation and leaves no regret . . ."

Furthermore, true repentance leads to a change in behavior, not just tears of regret.

Matthew 3:8, 10 "Produce fruit in keeping with repentance . . . The ax is already at the root of the trees, and every tree that does not produce good fruit will be cut down and thrown into the fire."

Remember, the heavenly Father stands prepared to kill the fatted calf at the first glimpse of us on the horizon, but it starts with repentance.

Free Indeed

At this point, a child of God with a repentant heart has the right to claim his freedom and no longer needs to be a slave to sin.

John 8:34 Jesus replied, "I tell you the truth, everyone who sins is a slave to sin. Now a slave has no permanent place in the family, but a son belongs to it forever. So if the Son sets you free, you will be free indeed."

You might be thinking to yourself, "This sounds good in theory, but I've done all you've said, and I don't feel free." Well, one of the titles given to the devil in Scripture is the "accuser of the brethren," and you can be sure that if you let him, he'll continue to remind you of who you used to be.

Revelation 12:10 "For the accuser of our brothers, who accuses them before our God day and night, has been hurled down."

He is like a wicked ex-slave master who can't have his slave back, so instead he reminds him every chance he gets that he was once a slave and he will never amount to anything more than a slave—a worthless, useless slave. But we are now royalty, children of the King, and we need to stop acting as if we are nothing more than slaves.

The Third Key–Prayer and Seeking God's Face

" . . . if my people . . . pray and seek my face . . ."

As children of the Father, set free by the Son through repentance, we may confidently approach God by seeking his face in prayer.

Hebrews 4:14–16 "Therefore, since we have a great high priest who has gone through the heavens, Jesus the Son of God, let us hold firmly to the faith we profess. For we do not have a high priest who is unable to sympathize with our weaknesses, but we have one who has been tempted in every way, just as we are—yet was without sin. **Let us then approach the throne of grace with confidence***, so that we may receive mercy and find grace to help us in our time of need." (emphasis added)*

What gives us the right to "approach the throne of grace with confidence"? In the times of the Old Testament, people could be put to death for approaching a king without having been summoned. Similarly, in the case of the tabernacle during the time of Moses all the way through to the temple during the life of Jesus, there was a thick curtain separating the "Most Holy Place" from the rest of the temple. The Ark of the Covenant was kept behind this curtain to signify that the presence of God should not be approached or treated with contempt. There had been those who had inadvertently come into contact with the Ark and perished for it. No one was allowed to enter the "Most Holy Place" except for the high priest, and only once per year with an offering of a blood sacrifice for sins. These restrictions were intended to emphasize the fact that the holiness of God, the heavenly King, should not be desecrated by the presence of sinful man, since there was no earthly sacrifice that could permanently atone for the sin of mankind.

I mention this because at the very moment Christ breathed his last breath on the cross,

Matthew 27:51 ". . . the curtain of the temple was torn in two from top to bottom."

The tearing of the curtain signaled that the death of Christ had permanently removed the barrier of sin between fallen humanity and our Holy God. All of Scripture had been pointing to this one moment: Our righteousness was made complete in Christ. Knowing this was to take place, Christ instructed his disciples to pray, beginning with "Our Father . . ." At the time, approaching the Almighty God with such familiarity would have been considered blasphemous. But now, through Christ and as God's children, we are told to approach Him as the heavenly Father.

Why do we pray if God already knows our thoughts?

Prayer is not simply a means to getting our needs met; it is an acknowledgment that God holds our lives and our futures in the palm His hand, and it is the primary vessel by which we are able to develop our relationship with Him. We don't pray to inform Him of things that have escaped His attention, but to express our need for His sovereign intervention. So prayer is a form of humility—a way of saying, "Lord, you are the Almighty God; you know my needs. I simply ask you to provide for them and for you to make your will known to me. Without you, my life is hopelessly out of control, and you alone can redeem it for your purposes."

Also, a good father will not simply lavish a continuous flow of gifts and provisions on his children, because this tends to breed complacency, greed and an immature sense of entitlement. In much the same way, God will only bless us materially as long as it does not hinder our relationship with Him—and even then, there are no guarantees.

Christmas-overload Syndrome

Anyone who has observed a child on Christmas morning who has gotten one-too-many gifts will be able to relate to this next story. You see, I have nine sisters (which might explain a lot to the reader), and up until the point when my siblings and I finally came to our senses, all of us had been buying gifts for each and every one of our nieces and nephews at Christmas time. It got to the point where the Chinese manufacturers were contacting us directly a few months early, just so they could get a jump on our orders. (The Chinese government becomes progressively more pro-Christian the closer you get to Christmas.) At one point, we decided it would be cheaper to just fly to China to pick up the toys rather than give Wal-Mart a chance to mark up the prices. So anyhow, as you can imagine, three weeks after the tree had been taken down, the kids were still opening up presents, and by that point you're hearing comments from the kids like, "Oh, great; another Quadra-Laser Full-Turbo Mega-Pump Water Blaster." Then, through clenched teeth and in hushed tones, you need to remind your child that their aunt stood in line at 4:30AM in the cold and was almost trampled by the angry Christmas shoppers to get that toy, which is now readily available for one third of the cost, "So try to show a little appreciation!"

Much to the dismay of the little children (and the Chinese), we have since adopted a grab-bag policy to help alleviate some of the holiday cheer hysteria, but the whole point to the story was this: Boycott China. No, actually the point was that God has no desire to cause us to resemble those spoiled children on Christmas, and prayer is one way of maintaining the recognition of our need for Him.

Summarizing the third key, we need to approach His throne of grace with confidence through prayer, knowing that He loved us enough to sacrifice His Son in order to make it possible for us to be called His children. And on a national level, we, as His children, are the only ones who have the right and the moral obligation to intercede on behalf of a sinful people. But as in the story of the prodigal son, we need to approach the Father with humility and reverence, and humility is most notably recognized by behavioral change—which leads us to the fourth key.

The Fourth Key–Change

" . . . if my people . . . turn from their wicked ways . . ."

Almost everyone has seen at least one of those end-of-the-world type movies in which the president is contacted and informed that he must make the ultimate decision to nuke the enemy. The camera will usually focus in on his jittery hands as he is given the secret envelope with the secret code, and inevitably there are two ominous looking keys which must be turned simultaneously in order to activate the nuclear weapon. In very much the same way, the secret to the powerful weapon of prayer—the third key—is held in the second and fourth keys being utilized together. And to extend the analogy, the first key—our position as children of the King—is what gives us the authority to turn the other two. The only way God responds to our prayers is when repentance (key 2) *and* change (key 4) precede our prayers.

> *Job 33:34 Should God then reward you on your own terms, when you refuse to repent?*

> *Acts 26:20 ". . . I preached that they should repent and turn to God and prove their repentance by their deeds. That is why the Jews seized me in the temple courts and tried to kill me."–Apostle Paul*

As you can see, the message of repentance and change is not a popular one, but it leads to a righteousness made possible through Christ; then our prayers will be effective.

> *Psalm 66:18–20 "If I had cherished sin in my heart, the Lord would not have listened; but God has surely listened and heard my voice in prayer. Praise be to God, who has not rejected my prayer or withheld his love from me!"*

> *James 5:16 "The prayer of a righteous man is powerful and effective."*

Removing the Shackles

Unfortunately, many Christians find themselves shackled as a result of their unceasing battles with the same areas of sin, and their witness to others is rendered ineffective.

I'll never forget the first time this point was driven home to me as a young Christian. I was in basic training for the army at the time, and as most people know, as a soldier you need to speak the language of a soldier. In other words, we learned that certain swear words were extremely versatile and could be used for a variety of emotions: happiness, sadness, anger, fatigue, commentary on the drill sergeants, etc. Now although I had become fluent in the military language, I was also leading a Bible study for my platoon, and I made no secret of the fact that I was a Christian.

I can't remember what the particular circumstance was, but on one occasion I was very angry about something, and I blurted out a stream of obscenities, which included taking the name of Jesus in vain in the worst possible way. A friend of mine, who was standing close by, just looked at me with great disappointment and asked, "You call yourself a Christian?" It never occurred to me that he was watching my life that closely, and it became a lesson that would be burned into my mind and heart for life.

Since I see the rising prominence of habitual sin as one of the primary threats to our Christian witness and to the modern Church, the next chapter will be sort of an expanded study of the fourth key—change. Many books have been written laying out a step-by-step approach to conquering sin patterns; so instead, I would like to study the war strategies of Satan in the four primary battlefields: the mind, heart, strength and soul. By doing this, it is my desire to reinforce the inspiration of others on the subject and to give a Biblical perspective on the issue of spiritual warfare.

CHAPTER 10
the four battlefields

The Mind, Heart, Strength and Soul

Hebrews 12:1–2 "Therefore, since we are surrounded by such a great cloud of witnesses, let us throw off everything that hinders and the sin that so easily entangles, and let us run with perseverance the race marked out for us. Let us fix our eyes on Jesus . . ."

Peanuts

As I began writing this chapter, I had what I consider a "Charlie Brown moment." By this, I don't mean as I was prepared to kick the spiritual football, God yanked it out, and I fell flat on my back. Nor do I mean you'll consider me a "blockhead" once you finish reading. Anyone who is a fan of "Peanuts" will remember a holiday special during which Charlie Brown goes to Lucy for psychiatric counseling, and in an effort to diagnose him, she presents him with the names of several different phobias. Finally, she gets to the last one called "pantophobia," and he asks, "What is pantophobia?" When Lucy explains that it is the fear of everything, the light goes on and he exclaims, "That's it!" and Lucy flips over backwards.

Well, I had a "That's it!" moment as I began studying Scripture for this chapter. I started writing with a rough idea of the direction I wanted to take, but I needed some Scripture references to lend credibility to my experience. Originally, I was going to examine three areas where I have personally witnessed the most obvious attack from the enemy—the mind, heart and soul. As I began searching for passages containing those three words, I noticed that very often they appeared side by side in the verses I read. And finally, as I read *Mark 12:29–30*, the proverbial light came on and I said, "That's it!" Just before these two verses, Jesus had been asked by a teacher of the law to give his opinion on which commandment was the greatest.

> *"The most important one," answered Jesus, "is this: 'Hear, O Israel, the Lord our God, the Lord is one. Love the Lord your God with all your **heart** and with all your **soul** and with all your **mind** and with all your **strength**.'" (emphasis added)*

Then it all became clear; if this is the greatest commandment, it stands to reason that the four areas mentioned in this commandment are the most likely points of attack by the enemy. And furthermore, all throughout Scripture, loving God is equated with obeying God, so if by attacking these four areas the devil can coerce us to disobey God and consequently show a lack of love for Him, he has accomplished his goal of getting us to break the greatest commandment.

With this in mind, we'll be studying Satan's strategies of assault on these four aspects of our being. His ultimate goal is to win on the battlefield of the soul, but if that is out of reach, he'll settle for less significant victories against the mind, heart or strength.

Although it is true to say that the outcome of the final war has been predetermined through the victory of the Cross, the reality is the individual battles continue to rage, and very much is still at stake. The stakes include: the life of the Church, our witness to others, the salvation of family, friends and acquaintances, the health of our marriages, and the list goes on. Now, since the battle usually begins with the mind, we'll begin there as well.

The Battlefield of the Mind

I say that the battle usually begins with the mind because every day our minds take in and process a continuous barrage of information from our culture, which is typically designed to appeal to our most base tendencies. Our senses and emotions present us with sights and sounds and scents and feelings, all of which cause a reaction of some sort—some innocent and some not so innocent. Our God-given desires act to unlock the gateway of the mind, and our adversary uses these desires—coupled with our sin nature—to gain a foothold. When we take steps to turn back the battle at this gateway, we begin to experience the strength of God.

Isaiah 28:6 He will be . . . a source of strength to those who turn back the battle at the gate.

As an example, let's revisit the account of Adam and Eve. One of the first things the serpent does is attack the mind of Eve by challenging her recollection of God's command.

Genesis 3:1 "Did God really say, 'You must not eat from any tree in the garden'?"

Now, the serpent knew this was a distortion of God's command, but it was his way of engaging Eve in a debate over God's sovereignty and motives. If we make the mistake of entertaining dialogue with the enemy, it is the first step to our downfall. "Did God really say that sex outside of marriage was wrong? Are you sure his intention wasn't just to keep our emotions from being hurt through promiscuity? After all, we are deeply committed to each other; surely he knows how in love we are. I could see if we had no intention of getting married . . . then, that would be more like sin."

As you can see, once we decide to make God's commands open for debate, the battle is practically lost. Once we abandon the sovereignty and omniscience of God, we can be certain that our sin nature is not going to rally on behalf of God. Without God, we find ourselves trying to match wits with Satan, armed with nothing but our limited human intellect.

> *Romans 1:21–22 "For although they knew God, they neither glorified him as God nor gave thanks to him, but their thinking became futile and their foolish hearts were darkened. Although they claimed to be wise, they became fools . . ."*

As I said earlier, the more secular our society becomes—and the more deeply entrenched the teachings of moral relativism become—the easier it becomes for Satan to win the battle of the mind. As the Scripture above would indicate, the moral wisdom of a nation is directly proportional to the level of acknowledgement of God and inversely proportional to that nation's perceived intellectual and philosophical prowess. In other words, the higher our intellectual noses are in the air, the less able we are to smell the stench of the moral slime in which we are standing. The wiser we think we are, the more stupider we become.

> *1 Corinthians 1:18–21, 25, 27* **For the message of the cross is foolishness to those who are perishing, but to us who are being saved it is the power of God.** *For it is written: "I will destroy the wisdom of the wise; the intelligence of the intelligent I will frustrate." Where is the wise man? Where is the scholar? Where is the philosopher of this age? Has not God made foolish the wisdom of the world? For since in the wisdom of God the world through its wisdom did not know him, God was pleased through the foolishness of what was preached to save those who believe . . . For the foolishness of God is wiser than man's wisdom, and the weakness of God stronger than man's strength . . . But God chose the foolish things of the world to shame the wise; God chose the weak things of the world to shame the strong. (emphasis added)*

At the time, the people of Corinth were deeply into Greek culture and placed a high premium on Greek philosophy and wisdom.

Knowing his audience, Paul focuses on a message of spiritual wisdom and says, "The message of the cross is foolishness to those who are perishing . . ." Isn't this the attitude we are continuously confronted with from the institutes of *higher* learning around the world? Christianity is one of the few groups remaining that may be openly ridiculed and impugned for being foolish and "intolerant," which is a code word for "they have beliefs which we, the enlightened, should not tolerate."

Psalm 53:1 The fool says in his heart—there is no God!

As the message of the cross becomes increasingly more foolish to our society, it follows that more and more people will be counted among "those who are perishing" eternally. Do you see why this battlefield of the mind is so crucial to Satan? Studies have shown that a vast majority of adult Christians actually became followers of Christ at a very young age. It is no wonder that this secular attack on the mind begins with the little children in elementary school. Also, for "those who are perishing"—those without Christ—the mind is often the only hurdle to habitual sin, hence, Satan's plan to capture it early. (Of course, there is that little thing called the conscience, but that can be slowly killed off with persistence.) The more people find themselves trapped by habitual sin, the more they feel obligated to be more tolerant of that particular sin in others and consequently, in the Church.

But thanks be to God, as Christians we have been given the mind of Christ, through his Spirit; it is a secret wisdom that is out of reach to those who wish to attain it through any other means but Christ.

1 Corinthians 2:4–9 "My message and my preaching were not with wise and persuasive words, but with a demonstration of the Spirit's power, **so that your faith might not rest on men's wisdom, but on God's power.** *We do, however, speak a message of wisdom among the mature, but not the wisdom of this age or of the rulers of this age, who are coming to nothing. No, we*

> *speak of **God's secret wisdom**, a wisdom that is hidden and that God designed for our glory before time began. None of the rulers of this age understood it, for if they had, they would not have crucified the Lord of glory. However, as it is written: 'No eye has seen, no ear has heard, no mind has conceived what God has prepared for those who love him'—but God has revealed it to us by his Spirit." (emphasis added)*

The Sword and the Trainer

Knowing that we are in a spiritual battle for the mind, we need to be continually reminded to use spiritual weapons, not just practical habits. As Christians, if we wait until the start of the battle to begin training with these weapons, we will be slaughtered. Say, for example, I am going into battle against a well trained, hardened warrior, and as I approach him, he notices a nice crisp sheath on my sword. Then as he advances, I glare at him with the most warrior-like expression I can muster, and I slowly unsheathe my sword, revealing an unblemished shiny weapon with the "Zechariah's Ironwerx" tag still attached. Understandably embarrassed, I nervously try to cut off the tag, but by that time, my fate is sealed.

That was a silly example, but it is not all that different from the approach to spiritual warfare we often employ. I've heard it said, "The condition of a person's spiritual life is inversely related to the condition of his Bible." We have been given the Sword of the Spirit—Holy Scripture—to help us wage war against Satan in the battlefield of the mind, so we need to train with it daily and vigorously.

> *2 Corinthians 10:4–6 The weapons we fight with are not the weapons of the world. On the contrary, they have divine power to demolish strongholds. We demolish arguments and every pretension that sets itself up against the knowledge of God, and we take captive every thought to make it obedient to Christ."*

the four battlefields

One very important detail we must not overlook is the need for a spiritual trainer, which has been given to us in the person of the Holy Spirit. Without the Holy Spirit, a well-intentioned reader of Scripture will not understand much of what is written. Additionally, not only does the Holy Spirit train us, but sometimes He sends us out to help train others. In the book of Acts, we read the account of the Ethiopian, who was sitting in his chariot reading the book of Isaiah. At this point in the story, he had not yet become a believer in Christ, so he was having difficulty making sense of what was written. At the same time, Philip was told by the Holy Spirit to "Go to the chariot and stay near it."

> *Acts 8:30–31 Then Philip ran up to the chariot and heard the man reading Isaiah the prophet. "Do you understand what you are reading?" Philip asked.*
>
> *"How can I," he said, "unless someone explains it to me?" So he invited Philip to come up and sit with him.*

As it turns out (not by chance), the Ethiopian was reading a prophecy by Isaiah predicting the suffering of the Christ. Philip proceeded to share with him "the good news about Jesus," and shortly after that, the Ethiopian asked to be baptized into Christ.

One thing to note about the Ethiopian was his humble response to Philip when he was asked if he understood what he was reading. His response could have been, "What do I look like, a Samaritan? Of course I understand it." But because he was willing to set his pride aside and ask for help, he is now spending eternity with Christ.

The Example of Christ

In the battlefield of the mind, the best example we can follow is the one set forth by Christ. Each time he was tempted by Satan in the desert, rather than engage the devil in a debate, he responded with "It is written . . ." It was an example that He intended for us to follow: Make Scripture your first line of defense when you are tempted. Also, we must be so familiar with Scripture that Satan is unable to twist it to his advantage.

> *Joshua 1:7–8 "Be strong and very courageous. Be careful to obey all the Law my servant Moses gave to you; do not turn from it to the right or to the left, that you may be successful wherever you go. Do not let this Book of the Law depart from your mouth; meditate on it day and night, so that you may be careful to do everything written in it. Then you will be prosperous and successful."*

Do not lay down your sword! It has been given to you as your primary weapon against the adversary, and if you are willing, the Holy Spirit will train you to use it properly.

The Battlefield of the Heart

Once the mind is either firmly within the grasp of Satan or he considers it out of reach, he goes for the heart. Returning to the example of Eve, the serpent continues his deception by questioning God's integrity:

> *Genesis 3:4–5 "You will not surely die," the serpent said to the woman. "For God knows that when you eat of it your eyes will be opened, and you will be like God, knowing good and evil."*

So now, Eve begins to question God's love and concern for her; she's wondering, "Why would he want to keep something so beautiful from me, unless the serpent is right and he has something to hide? Wow . . . I wonder what it would be like to have the ultimate power of God—to know good from evil (whatever that is)." She went from feeling betrayed by God (betrayal of the heart) to wanting God's wisdom (corruption of the heart).

Isn't this the way it usually happens in our lives? We say things like, "God, I don't understand why you would want to keep me from the joy of being married, but if you don't do something soon, I'm no longer going to play the part of the poor, innocent, single person." "God, you know our financial picture. As a matter of fact, I'm not so sure you didn't cause it, so forgive me if I take matters into my own hands." "God, you know I've always wanted children. If you can't do something as simple as that for me, do you really expect me to serve you with my life?" "God, you asked me to be open to having another child, and I was. Now you have taken that child from me. Is this the way you treat your children?" "God, every day I pray for my children, and yet now my little girl is pregnant. Am I supposed to thank you for that also?"

Obviously, having an intellectual discussion about protecting your heart and actually living it out in real life are two different things. The depths of the human heart are beyond our ability to grasp, but the importance of the heart to Christ and to our eternal glory can not be overstated.

> *Proverbs 4:23–27 Above all else, guard your heart, for it is the wellspring of life.*
> *- Put away perversity from your mouth; keep corrupt talk far from your lips.*
> *- Let your eyes look straight ahead, fix your gaze directly before you.*
> *- Make level paths for your feet and take only ways that are firm.*

"Above all else . . ." is pretty strong phrasing, especially given the numerous weighty issues covered in the book of Proverbs. Christ taught that to sin in your heart was just as much of a sin as carrying it out. He was raising the bar for all of the self-righteous spiritual leaders of the time, who outwardly obeyed all the legalistic religious laws but in their hearts, they were corrupt.

> *Luke 11:39–41 Then Jesus said to him, "Now then, you Pharisees clean the outside of the cup and dish, but inside you are full of greed and wickedness. You foolish people! Did not the One who made the outside make the inside also? But give what is inside the dish to the poor, and everything will be clean for you."*

Also, He taught that our actions reflect what is truly in our hearts:

Matthew 15:18–20 "But the things that come out of the mouth come from the heart, and these make a man 'unclean.' For out of the heart come evil thoughts, murder, adultery, sexual immorality, theft, false testimony, slander. These are what make a man 'unclean.'"

Reading the passage above, it becomes obvious why the human heart—the very essence of our being and emotions—is a far greater prize to Satan than the mind. Out of a corrupt heart flows every type of human depravity known to mankind. I say it is a greater prize because I believe it is possible to intellectually believe and understand the commands of God while simultaneously continuing a lifestyle of sin, because of the corrupt nature of our hearts. Adam and Eve sinned, not because they didn't believe in the existence of God, but because they believed God had betrayed them by keeping something good from them. Their limited human intelligence did not understand something about God's nature or His commands regarding sin, death and eternity, so rather than trust the Almighty, they chose to play God and make their own rules.

Isaiah 55:8 "For my thoughts are not your thoughts, neither are your ways my ways," declares the Lord.

An Electric Moment

Don't tell my dad, but when I was about twelve or thirteen I decided to test some of the laws of electricity, which I knew existed, but I didn't fully respect. Something inside me asked, "Did your dad ever really say, 'Don't cut the cord off an old lamp and separate the wires, and *definitely* don't plug in the cord and proceed to connect a pair of pliers to the exposed wires'?" Fortunately, I was bright enough (if I may say that) to use a pair of pliers with insulated grips, and I

the four battlefields

survived the explosion. (Dad, if you are reading this, I was going to replace the pliers.) If family members had come looking for me, I could have asked, "Did you not know that I would be in my father's garage testing the laws of physics?"

Oddly enough, I became a trained electrician in the army, and now I have a healthy respect for those little copper wires. But isn't this much like Adam and Eve's experience? They knew God's power was not to be toyed with, but the temptation to test that power overrode their God-given sensibilities, and they paid a hefty price for the rest of their natural lives, ending with death.

For the devoted Christian whose mind is firmly rooted in Scripture, the primary battlefield becomes the heart. In this fallen state, life inevitably carries many sorrows and disappointments, so the enemy challenges God's love for us by getting us to dwell on these things. This has been the story since the beginning of time, and the Bible makes no attempt to gloss it over:

Psalm 13:1–2 "How long, O Lord? Will you forget me forever? How long will you hide your face from me? How long must I wrestle with my thoughts and every day have sorrow in my heart?"

In this passage, the psalmist obviously has a deep relationship with the Lord, but he feels betrayed. When you read this verse, you'll notice the psalmist fighting the battle in his *mind* and in his *heart*. In many ways, Scripture portrays the heart as being fickle at best and deceitful at worst:

Jeremiah 17:9–10 "The heart is deceitful above all things and beyond cure. Who can understand it?"

But strangely enough, it is often the mind—when transformed by the Holy Spirit—which becomes our ally, even as the heart is wavering.

Romans 12:2 ". . . be transformed by the renewing of your mind. Then you will be able to test and approve what God's will is—His good, pleasing and perfect will."

It is an intriguing cycle: Satan first attempts to use the mind to keep us from choosing Christ, but Christ fills our hearts with His love and His Holy Spirit and the heart overrides the mind as we accept His invitation, making us sons and daughters of the living God. Then Satan attacks our hearts and our devotion to God by challenging His love for us. But if our mind is being transformed and renewed by His Spirit and through Scripture, we will stand firm on what we know about God's character as a loving and perfect Father. Ultimately, our faith is strengthened through this whole process, and we begin taking on the likeness of Christ, which acts as a witness to someone else's heart—and the cycle begins again.

The purity of heart, which results from surrendering our mind and our will to God, allows us to see Him and take on His likeness.

Matthew 5:8 "Blessed are the pure in heart for they will see God."

The Example of Christ

Once again, the example of Christ becomes the most profound lesson we can learn when contemplating the battlefield of the heart. His struggle on the cross is graphically depicted in Psalm 22, which might seem odd since the book of Psalms was written approximately 1000 years before Christ walked the Earth. Now, some might think Christ was quoting Psalm 22 while on the cross, but it was actually the reverse. Just as many prophets predicted the birth and birthplace of the Messiah, Psalm 22 prophesies the graphic nature of His suffering and also the words He would use to express His anguish.

Psalm 22:1, 2, 7, 8, 16–18 **My God, my God, why have you forsaken me?** *Why are you so far from saving me, so far from the words of my groaning? O my God, I cry out by day, but you* *do not answer, by night, and am not silent . . . All who see me mock me; they hurl insults, shaking their heads: "He trusts in the Lord; let the Lord rescue him. Let him deliver him, since he delights in him." . . . Dogs have surrounded me; a band of evil men has encircled me,* **they have pierced my hands and my feet.** *I can count all my bones; people stare and gloat over me. They divide my garments among them and cast lots for my clothing.* (emphasis added)

Imagine—1000 years before Christ, the nature of His suffering on the cross having been so accurately prophesied. Do you suppose the guards were standing around asking each other, "What do you think we should do next?" "Well Psalm 22 says we should pierce his hands and feet, cast lots for his clothing, and then taunt him about trusting in God, at which point he's supposed to yell, 'My God, my God, why have you forsaken me?' But we need to make sure we stick him in the side with a spear instead of breaking his legs like the other two criminals, because there is another Scripture that says none of his bones will be broken."

As heart wrenching as Psalm 22 is, in a strange sort of way it should provide comfort, because its prophetic nature shows that life is not as haphazard and out-of-control as it seems. Each and every one of our days was numbered before we were even conceived.

Keeping this in mind, when our heart is under attack by Satan or just by life circumstances, we must continually remind ourselves that we have a Savior who—being fully aware of what he was about to suffer—chose the torture of the cross to make it possible for us to be called sons and daughters of God. When Christ was in anguish in the Garden of Gethsemane, it was obvious that the devil was attacking his heart with so much darkness and oppression that it caused him to sweat drops of blood. And He prayed,

Matthew 26:39 "My Father, if it is possible, may this cup be taken from me. Yet not as I will, but as you will."

This is a picture of complete surrender. Although He had the right and the power to stop Himself from being tortured, He forfeited that right and allowed Himself to feel and experience the most extreme suffering that any human could ever experience. As I mentioned earlier, the worst part of the suffering He endured was the feeling of betrayal and abandonment. (Just don't ask me how it was possible for Jesus to feel forsaken by the Father. We'll never be able to understand what was happening in the spiritual realms to allow Jesus to continue being God, the Son, yet to experience the human emotion of feeling abandoned by God, the Father.) Although He had not been abandoned, the feeling of abandonment was real—"My God, my God, why have you forsaken me?"

Many people might believe a question like that is near blasphemous. But what it should say to us is that Christ did not secretly hold on to some of His miraculous powers, being the Son of God, to help alleviate some of the anguish and pain He would experience. This was a fully human response to the spiritual, physical and emotional suffering He was going through. "My God, my God, why have you forsaken me?" Yet, it was an act of obedience that put him there. "Yet not as I will, but as you will."

His example to us, in this battle for the heart, is this: In times of despair, we must place all of our pain, heartache, doubts, feelings of betrayal and disappointment at the foot of the cross and say, "Yet not as I will, but as You will."

The Lord is My Shepherd

It is no coincidence that a Psalm depicting anguish, Psalm 22, would be followed by a Psalm of encouragement, Psalm 23. I will go out on a limb and suggest that Psalm 23 is meant to be a follow-up prophecy to Psalm 22, and that it is an actual representation of what Christ experienced as he emerged from the tomb, victorious over death.

Psalm 23 The Lord is my shepherd, I shall not be in want. He makes me lie down in green pastures, he leads me beside quiet waters, he restores my soul. He guides me in paths of righteousness for his name's sake. Even though I walk through the valley of the shadow of death, I will fear no evil, for you are with me; your rod and your staff, they comfort me. You prepare a table before me in the presence of my enemies. You anoint my head with oil; my cup overflows. Surely goodness and love will follow me all the days of my life, and I will dwell in the house of the Lord forever.

The Battlefield of Strength

Something worth pointing out as we study the different battlefields is that they are unavoidably linked, and the battlefield of strength is no different. The two examples of temptation I used in reference to Christ were the only two scenarios in Scripture in which Christ is being tempted and harassed by Satan. The first was His temptation in the desert, and the second was His anguish in the garden leading up to His crucifixion.

The most conspicuous similarity between both scenarios is that Christ was exhausted—either physically, spiritually or emotionally—and the devil attempted to use this to his advantage. Being fully human in terms of the physical body, after fasting for forty days He was famished, and at that point Satan tempts Him to turn the stones into bread. After tempting Him twice more, Luke 4:13 says that the devil "left him until an opportune time," which would be three years later in the garden of Gethsemane. In this case, He was emotionally and spiritually exhausted from contemplating the crucifixion, and the demonic torment would continue all the way through to His actual physical torture and death.

If this was Satan's strategy in the temptation of Jesus, how much more will it be his strategy with us? Say, for example, you are a businessman exhausted from a long trip and all you want to do is to sit in your hotel room with some mindless entertainment. It is just a matter of time before you find yourself carelessly flipping through channels and your mindless entertainment turns to godless entertainment. You might say, "It's just a harmless, guilty pleasure." But Christ has set the standard a little higher than that:

Matthew 5:27, 31 "You have heard it said, 'Do not commit adultery.'... But I tell you that anyone who looks at a woman lustfully has already committed adultery with her in his heart."
- Jesus

Now add to the physical exhaustion some emotional exhaustion from a struggling marriage, and the temptation to get a little bit of emotional counseling from the opposite sex is amplified. Now add in an element of spiritual exhaustion from a long held grudge against God for letting you get into this mess in the first place, and victory for Satan is all but assured.

Addiction

Not only do many marriages begin to fail this way, but many addictions are formed under these conditions as well. This is relevant when talking about the battlefield of strength, because addictions sap our strength and resources and cause us to do things we wouldn't otherwise do. Any time the adversary can get us to be completely or partially reliant on something other than God, sin is knocking at the door. Just about everyone has witnessed friends and loved ones completely destroy themselves and their families as a result of all sorts of addictions. Very often it starts as just a crutch—a coping mechanism to get you through a tough spot. Before you know it, you find yourself being secretive, followed by the realization that it takes more and more to satisfy the addiction. Eventually, your love for God and your family is not enough to help you overcome the addiction. At this point it takes either divine intervention or hospitalization—or both.

Sin is always progressive because we have an enemy who desires to destroy us and our families and our churches. When we are told to love the Lord our God with all of our strength, it partially means doing whatever is necessary to overcome addiction and habitual sin. It means putting God and others above yourself and fighting sin with every ounce of energy you can muster.

The Example of Christ

> *Hebrews 12:2–4 "**Let us fix our eyes on Jesus,** the author and perfecter of our faith, who for the joy set before him endured the cross, scorning its shame, and sat down at the right hand of the throne of God. Consider him who endured such opposition from sinful men, so that you will not grow weary and lose heart. **In your struggle against sin, you have not yet resisted to the point of shedding your blood.**" (emphasis added)*

Christ resisted sin to the point of shedding His blood for us; this needs to be our standard. In this age of material comfort and unbridled desire for entertainment, it is difficult to get our minds around something so noble and right. Built into every person, I believe, is a deep down desire to do something noble—to fight for a just cause—to live for something bigger than ourselves. But unless a house is burning down or a child is trapped in a well, everyday modern life provides very little opportunity to do something tangibly noble.

I believe that if we could visibly see the spiritual battle going on around us, we would recognize that the time to be noble and heroic is now—right where we are. To each of us it means something different, but to all of us it means loving the Lord our God with all of our strength. This might mean fighting addiction, or forgiving someone, or loving our families, or serving our fellow man, or giving of our time, talents and resources. Satan renders us useless in these areas if we allow him to sap our strength physically, spiritually, psychologically or emotionally. But we have a God who deeply desires to provide the strength we need, if we will let Him.

Isaiah 40:29–31 He gives strength to the weary and increases the power of the weak. Even youths grow tired and weary, and young men stumble and fall; but those who hope in the Lord will renew their strength. They will soar on wings like eagles; they will run and not grow weary, they will walk and not be faint.

Matthew 11:28–29 "Come to me, all you who are weary and burdened, and I will give you rest. Take my yoke upon you and learn from me, for I am gentle and humble in heart, and you will find rest for your souls. For my yoke is easy and my burden is light."—Jesus

Only when we learn to "fix our eyes on Jesus" and surrender to Him all of life's burdens will we learn to "soar on wings like eagles."

The Battlefield of the Soul

Because of the fleeting nature of this life compared to eternity, the soul is the primary battlefield on which every other battle is fought. For example, what does it matter, ultimately, if you win a battle against an addiction but you spend eternity in hell? You could ask the same question about saving your marriage, or fighting for freedom, or finding a cure for AIDS, or saving the planet. Yes, all of these things will better the plight of humanity and increase our quality of life here on earth, but for what ultimate purpose? Don't misunderstand, all of these things are noble causes, and God blesses specific people with the intelligence and persistence and passion to champion them, but still, every life boils down to the moment of death.

Matthew 16:25–26 "For whoever wants to save his life will lose it, but whoever loses his life for me and for the gospel will save it. What good is it for a man to gain the whole world, yet forfeit his soul? Or what can a man give in exchange for his soul?—Jesus

The implication is obvious; there is nothing we can give in ex-

the four battlefields

change for our soul, so this is one battle we had better not lose. As I said in chapter three, there is only one way to be assured of victory on the battlefield of the soul—it is through the blood of the Lamb who was slain in order to cleanse us from sin, presenting us to the Father clothed in a garment of righteousness.

For Satan to win this battle for our souls, he will relentlessly attack on the other three fronts. He will attack our minds to get us to doubt God's commands, His judgment, His fairness, His truth and even His existence. Satan will attack our hearts to get us to doubt God's love for us, His concern for our welfare and His provision for us. And finally, he will attack our strength to wear us down to the point where we give up the fight against sin, addiction and injustice.

This all may sound overwhelming, but we do not serve a God who is helpless or indifferent. We serve a mighty God who created us for *His* glory, and *He* will go before us into battle; at the sound of His voice, heaven and earth will bow down.

> *Psalm 46:1–3, 6, 7, 10, 11 God is our refuge and strength, an ever-present help in trouble. Therefore we will not fear, though the earth give way and the mountains fall into the heart of the sea, though its waters roar and foam and the mountains quake with their surging . . . Nations are in uproar, kingdoms fall; He lifts his voice, the earth melts. The Lord almighty is with us; the God of Jacob is our fortress . . .* **Be still, and know that I am God;** *I will be exalted among the nations, I will be exalted in the earth.* **The Lord almighty is with us;** *the God of Jacob is our fortress. (emphasis added)*

Heal Our Land

Once we are committed to this battle against sin, as God's people we have the right to expect Him to come and "heal our land." We must take the promises of Scripture to be literal covenants, not empty promises, and if we obey God and His commands, I still believe we will see His mercy. Up to this point in history, with all of its flaws, our great nation has been a place of refuge for those seeking religious freedom, but this freedom is rapidly being eroded. Those who believe that God has a particular standard for morality and righteousness are constantly berated as intolerant Neanderthals (not that there is anything wrong with that). But still, America was founded on the Judeo-Christian ethic, and so far, this is still a land in which we can openly worship without being tortured or shot.

The Greatest Commandment

In the beginning of this chapter, I mentioned that we are told by the first commandment to love God with all of our heart, soul, mind and strength; if we were to obey just this one commandment, our nation would be changed from the inside out. Beyond what I have already mentioned about battling sin, there are many ways to live out this commandment in practical, real life terms, and I believe this is the key to shifting our nation back toward righteousness.

The remainder of this book will be devoted to inspiring each Christian to reach deep down to the core of his or her being to stir up whatever passion has been left dormant, with the purpose of helping direct that passion toward the reclaiming of America for Christ, our Captain.

CHAPTER 11
the remnant

"I am the only one left . . ."

In the book of 1 Kings, chapter 19, we find Elijah running from Jezebel, the wife of King Ahab; she had threatened to kill him for putting to death all the prophets of Baal. After traveling for forty days and forty nights, Elijah takes cover inside of a cave, where the Lord questions him:

> *1 Kings 19:13–14 Then a voice said to him, "What are you doing here, Elijah?" He replied, "I have been very zealous for the Lord God Almighty. The Israelites have rejected your covenant, broken down your altars, and put your prophets to death with the sword. I am the only one left, and now they are trying to kill me too."*

The Lord proceeds to give some instruction to Elijah and then reassures him that he is not the only one left who is willing to serve God:

> *v. 18 "Yet I reserve seven thousand in Israel—all whose knees have not bowed down to Baal and all whose mouths have not kissed him."*

Later in Scripture (in the book of Romans), the Apostle Paul recounts this very story to encourage the believers, telling them they were part of a chosen remnant set aside to carry on the faith in the face of a Church in great turmoil.

> *Romans 11:5–6 "So too, at the present time there is a remnant chosen by grace. And if it is by grace, then it is no longer by works; if it were, grace would no longer be grace."*

And so too, at this present time, I believe there is a remnant comprised of those who have refused to bow down to the secular culture and who desire to see righteousness back in the places of authority. As I write, I am reading a book about the founding fathers of our nation entitled *Under God*, by Toby Mac and Michael Tait. It is a compilation of quotes and stories about the men and women who suffered great injustices and even death for the sake of freedom. I am absolutely amazed at how much detail has been purged from our history books regarding faith and God, all in the name of tolerance.

Under God contains a story about the life of Patrick Henry, and to my shame, all I've known about him up to this point was his quote, "Give me liberty or give me death!" As it turns out, he was an extremely devout Christian who faithfully prayed for one hour each evening, followed by devotions with his family. Those heroic and patriotic words quoted above came from a speech given to the delegates at the Revolutionary Convention in Virginia, at which Virginians were debating their role in the American Revolution. I would like to quote the entire speech because of the similarities I see between the state of the nation at the time of Patrick Henry and the present-day state of the Christian Church. As is typically the case in politics, the vast majority of the delegates at the time of the Revolution were interested in the path of least resistance, and they believed Britain could still be appeased and reasoned with. Inspired by God, Patrick Henry launched into his speech, addressing the president of the convention:

> *Mr. President . . . Should I keep back my opinions at such a time, through fear of giving offense, I should consider myself as guilty of*

treason towards my country, and of an act of disloyalty toward the Majesty of Heaven, which I revere above all earthly kings.

Sir, we have done everything that could be done to avert the storm which is now coming on. There is no longer any room for hope. If we wish to be free . . . we must fight! An appeal to arms and to the God of hosts is all that is left us!

They tell us, sir, that we are weak . . . Sir, we are not weak... The millions of people, armed in the holy cause of liberty, and in such a country as we possess, are invincible by any force which our enemy can send against us.

Besides, sir, we shall not fight our battles alone. There is a just God who presides over the destinies of nations.

. . . The battle, sir, is not to the strong alone; it is to the vigilant, the active, the brave. Besides, sir . . . it is now too late to retire from the contest. There is no retreat but in submission and slavery! . . . The war is inevitable—and let it come! I repeat it sir, let it come . . .

The next gale that sweeps from the north will bring to our ears the clash of resounding arms! Our brethren are already in the field! Why stand we here idle? What is it that gentlemen wish? What would they have? Is life so dear, or peace so sweet, as to be purchased at the price of chains and slavery? Forbid it, Almighty God! I know not what course others may take; but as for me, give me liberty or give me death!

When I read this for the first time, everything about it said to me that this was a man of conviction and purpose. There was a calling on his life, and he made the most of it. The first sentence of his speech speaks volumes: "Mr. President . . . Should I keep back my opinions at such a time, through fear of giving offense . . ."

People were no different back then; no decent person wanted to offend his colleagues, or worse yet, sound like an alarmist. But there are times in history when men and women of honor and decency are called to step forward and face persecution for righteousness and freedom.

For me, this speech rings true because of the Spirit of God behind it. It was not puffed up gloating or pride; it was the very Spirit of God speaking through his servant. Patrick Henry considered it an act of treason against his country and disloyalty "toward the Majesty of Heaven" to keep quiet as God was urging him to speak up. Words like this only come from someone who was part of God's "remnant" for his time. Just as the Apostle Paul pointed out, this remnant is chosen by the grace of God, not simply by a person's desire to be remembered for something noble.

Now in many places throughout Scripture the word 'remnant' simply refers to those of God's people who have survived a great calamity of some sort. But for the purposes of this book, I will define the remnant as those who are left standing after a corrupt culture ravages the body of believers. These are the ones who stand defiantly in the face of ridicule and persecution for their beliefs and are responsible for keeping the spiritual torch lit for the next generation. Elijah believed he was the last remaining survivor of the faith, but the Lord informed him there were seven thousand others. And I would be willing to bet that each one of the seven thousand felt as if he, alone, was the last one remaining.

My goal is not to heap guilt on those who have a difficult time just trying to make it from one day to the next, let alone entertaining any grandiose ideas about saving America. But my goal is to motivate those who have been inspired by God to take a stand for His kingdom and His righteousness and also to encourage those who sometimes feel as if they are one of the last remaining committed Christians.

Identifying the Remnant

If the remnant is chosen by grace, then it must be more a matter of identifying and rallying the remnant rather than recruiting members. To do this, I'd like to examine Patrick Henry's speech to get a glimpse into the character of someone who was a charter member of the remnant of his time.

Character Trait 1: As I mentioned earlier, Patrick Henry was a man of conviction who displayed a God-inspired passion to speak the truth regardless of the ridicule or disdain he might encounter for doing so. Those who are led by God are unable to contain their desire to speak His truth. To members of the remnant, the truth is not obscure or transient; as Thomas Jefferson wrote in The Declaration of Independence, "We hold these truths to be self-evident . . ."

Trait 2: Members of the remnant take no delight or personal pride in fighting the enemy, but when necessary, they will defend a holy and righteous cause. In the second paragraph of his speech, Patrick Henry points out, *"Sir, we have done everything to avert the storm, which is now coming on."* He had no more desire to go to war than anyone else, but he had the wisdom to know when it was time to act, and he saw it as his mission to inspire others to act as well.

Trait 3: Members of the remnant understand and believe in the cause for which they stand and are unwilling to allow the enemy to convince them that they are weak.

"Sir, we are not weak . . . The millions of people, armed in the holy cause of liberty . . ."

Trait 4: Members of the remnant stand firm in the fact that it is God who goes before them in battle, and it is God who will determine our ultimate destiny.

"There is a just God who presides over the destinies of nations."

Trait 5: For the remnant, vigilance and bravery outclass strength every time, but cowardice ends in slavery and submission to the enemy.

> "... The battle, sir, is not to the strong alone; it is to the vigilant, the active, the brave. Besides, sir ... it is now too late to retire from the contest. There is no retreat but in submission and slavery!"

Trait 6: Patrick Henry was repulsed by the idea of sitting around idle while others died for the cause, and he was firmly resolved to do what God called him to, regardless of the actions of others. Members of the remnant are willing to go to their deaths fighting for what they know to be right; literally, Christian martyrdom around the world is more frequent now than ever before.

> "The next gale that sweeps from the north will bring to our ears the clash of resounding arms! Our brethren are already in the field! Why stand we here idle? What is it that gentlemen wish? What would they have? Is life so dear, or peace so sweet, as to be purchased at the price of chains and slavery? Forbid it, Almighty God! I know not what course others may take; but as for me, give me liberty or give me death!"

Trait 7: The lives of the remnant produce results. Because of Patrick Henry's impassioned speech, Virginia voted to join Massachusetts in the fight for freedom and liberty, and the rest is history.

If it weren't for the conviction and bravery of godly men and women, this country would not exist, and the same is now true for the Church. If the remnant does not stand up and be identified and rally to the cause, our nation and the Church will continue to decline into oblivion.

For those of us who are inspired by men like Patrick Henry, the time to act on that inspiration is now; it makes no sense to stand around wringing our hands and wishing for the "good old days."

Ecclesiastes 7:10 Do not say, "Why were the old days better than these?" For it is not wise to ask such questions.

As you can see from this verse, even in the time of Solomon people were asking the question, "What happened to the good old days?" Rather than complain or turn a blind eye, we must seize the day and give it back to God, asking Him to make something worthwhile of it.

The Fall of Jerusalem

Around 450 B.C., there lived a man named Nehemiah, whose life was used by God to inspire the Jewish remnant that survived the fall of Jerusalem approximately ninety years earlier. (In this case, the remnant is simply defined as those who were not put to death by the king of Babylon.) Every time I read about Nehemiah in Scripture, I can't help but notice the striking similarities between his intense struggle to rebuild the walls of Jerusalem and our everyday struggle to live out the Christian faith.

To set the stage, Jerusalem was attacked by the king of Babylon, Nebuchadnezzar, and conquered in 586 B.C. The king thoroughly destroyed Jerusalem, burning the temple and breaking down the wall around the city to the point where almost nothing was left. Any of the Israelites who survived the siege were taken into captivity and became servants, and for seventy years this small remnant was in exile, unable to return to Jerusalem.

It is crucial to understand why the city was destroyed, if we are to continue to believe that God protects and provides for a righteous people. Eleven years before the fall of Jerusalem, King Zedekiah took the throne and ruled over the Israelites, but "He did evil in the eyes of the Lord his God and did not humble himself before Jeremiah the prophet, who spoke the word of the Lord." (2 Chronicles 36:12) As a result of his wicked leadership, sin became rampant in the city, and even the Church leaders became corrupt.

> *2 Chronicles 36:13–16 He (Zedekiah) became stiff-necked and hardened his heart and would not turn to the Lord, the God of Israel. Furthermore, all the leaders of the priests and the people became more and more unfaithful, following all the detestable practices of the nations and defiling the temple of the Lord, which he had consecrated in Jerusalem.*
>
> *The Lord, the God of their fathers, sent word to them through his messengers again and again, because he had pity on his people and on his dwelling place. But they mocked God's messengers, despised his words and scoffed at his prophets until the wrath of the Lord was aroused against his people and there was no remedy.*

Because of the sinful pride of the Israelites, God used the king of Babylon to destroy the holy city of Jerusalem. This tells us two things: First, God is more concerned about the holiness and obedience of His people than the sacred sites or buildings bearing His name. Second, God is not above using a godless ruler or nation to bring judgment upon His people.

Broken Walls

Seventy years after the fall, "the Lord moved the heart of Cyrus king of Persia," (Ezra 1:1) and he issued a proclamation allowing the exiled remnant of Israel to return to Jerusalem for the purpose of rebuilding the temple of the Lord. After many years and lots of resistance from their enemies, the temple was rebuilt, and they could finally worship God again in the temple at Jerusalem.

But the city was still without walls, leaving the Israelites vulnerable to their enemies, and this is where Nehemiah finally enters the picture. Nehemiah was cupbearer to Artaxerxes, King of Persia, and was among those who had been unable to return to Jerusalem to help rebuild it. The Lord gave him a passion to see Jerusalem restored, and

the remnant

so he inquired of a few men from Judah "about the Jewish remnant that survived the exile, and also about Jerusalem." (Nehemiah 1:2)

> *Nehemiah 1:3–4 They said to me, "Those who survived the exile and are back in the province are in great trouble and disgrace. The wall of Jerusalem is broken down, and its gates have been burned with fire."*
>
> *When I heard these things, I sat down and wept. For some days I mourned and fasted and prayed before the God of heaven."*

Much like Patrick Henry's passion for this land we now enjoy, Nehemiah was wholeheartedly devoted to Jerusalem and God's people, and he was moved to tears to find out about its wretched condition. The Christian remnant in America needs to be just as heartbroken about the state of the Church and our country. The enemy has broken down our walls, and our gates have been burned.

Just as an example, the other day I read a story in *USA Today* about a game that school children are now playing sometimes called "flat-liner" or "suffocation roulette," during which children choke each other with ropes or towels or even their own hands. The object of the game is to get a rush from coming as close as possible to death without actually dying; many have already been strangled to death. When our children become this lost, this devoid of hope, this desperate for a thrill or even just to fit in, it should move us to tears, and if it doesn't, there is nothing left but the "fearful prospect of judgment."

Reading an article like that should sadden and frustrate each one of us, but it should also cause us to be moved by the Holy Spirit to mourning and prayer, as Nehemiah was—and then to action. The first thing Nehemiah did after his period of mourning was to offer up to God a prayer of repentance for his own sins and for the sins of the people of Jerusalem. There was not an ounce of self-righteousness; just repentance and a broken heart.

Each one of us has fallen short in some way and has not done everything possible to prevent the current state of chaos in our nation, so repentance should always be the first step in the rebuilding process. But from here—the point of repentance—we must begin the rebuilding process.

Rebuilding the Walls

Even though Nehemiah sensed the calling of God to rebuild the walls of Jerusalem, he faced a number of obstacles to this task, not the least of which was his position of servitude to the king. But God was already working in the heart of the king, so Nehemiah was able to convince Artaxerxes to let him return to Jerusalem to oversee the work. This is the most important aspect of Christian service—the realization that it is Jesus our Captain who goes out ahead of us to ensure success. In a way, it is sort of like the father who pretends as if he is struggling to remove the lid from a jar, and as he loosens it slightly, he hands it to his five-year-old son and says, "Here, I need you to help me open it." The boy pops off the lid and runs around saying, "I did it! I did it! And daddy couldn't!"

This is not to imply everything will be easy. Nehemiah was given a vision—a vision to rebuild the walls—but as you might expect, there were people ready and willing to criticize the vision. When Nehemiah shared his vision with the remnant, they replied:

> *Nehemiah 2:18–20 "Let us start rebuilding." So they began this good work.*
>
> *But when Sanballat the Horonite, Tobiah the Ammonite official and Geshem the Arab heard about it, they mocked and ridiculed us. "What is this you are doing?" they asked. "Are you rebelling against the king?"*
>
> *I answered them by saying, "The God of heaven will give us success. We his servants will start rebuilding, but as for you, you have no share in Jerusalem or any claim or historic right to it."*

What a great answer; essentially he told them, "You're not part of the remnant, so I wouldn't expect you to understand." Don't expect everyone to enthusiastically jump up and down when you share your vision with them. On the contrary, it is more likely to be met with a collective yawn and a glazing over of the eyes. Even within the Church there are people who will fight against God's will every chance they get. In the *Parable of the Weeds*, Jesus tells a story about a farmer who had an enemy sneak in and sow weeds in his field. The farmer's servants asked him if he wanted the weeds pulled up, but he told them not to, because some of the wheat could accidentally be pulled up with the weeds.

In the parable, the field represents the world, but it could just as easily represent the Church, because there are people within the Church who don't belong there and have actually been planted by the enemy. But it would do more harm than good for God's servants to try to weed them out, so we should leave the weeding to Him, for when He returns to judge the world. In other words, don't sit in church thinking to yourself, "He's a weed, she's a weed, he's not a weed . . ." It is enough to realize the weeds exist, and because they are planted by the enemy, they will resist any rebuilding efforts. But don't assume all resistance is evil; it might just be God trying to redirect your efforts. On a number of occasions I thought I knew for certain God's will in regard to my service within the Church, but then the door would slam shut, and I'd be back to square one. But with prayer and humility, His will eventually becomes clear.

Somebody get the weed-whacker.

Anyway, back to Nehemiah. As the work began to progress and the wall of Jerusalem rose from the ashes, the attacks intensified.

> *Nehemiah 4:1–3 When Sanballat heard that we were rebuilding the wall, he became angry and was greatly incensed. He ridiculed the Jews, and in the presence of his associates and the army of Samaria, he said, "What are these feeble Jews doing?*

Will they restore their wall? Will they offer sacrifices? Will they finish in a day? Can they bring the stones back to life from those heaps of rubble—burned as they are?"

Tobiah the Ammonite, who was at his side, said, "What are they building—if even a fox climbed up on it, he would break down their wall of stones!"

This sounds more like a scene from a playground than anything else, but eventually the verbal abuse escalates to threats of terrorism, and discouragement starts to set in.

Nehemiah 4:10–11 Meanwhile, the people in Judah said, "The strength of the laborers is giving out, and there is so much rubble that we cannot rebuild the wall." Also our enemies said, "Before they know it or see us, we will be right there among them and will kill them and put an end to the work."

Serving God is not always gloriously leaping from one victory to the next. There will always come a point at which we will ask ourselves, "Is this really worth it?" Anything worth fighting for comes at a great cost—physically, financially, spiritually, emotionally, etc. According to the book *Under God*, there was a point at which the revolution almost failed because the soldiers hadn't been paid, and their families were starving. The men were ready to give up the fight, but God inspired Robert Morris to take up the cause of finding the money necessary to essentially finance the revolution.

Nehemiah's mission to rebuild the wall reached a similar point; his workers were tired and hungry, and their families were under the threat of attack. But he encouraged them in a style very similar to Patrick Henry's:

Nehemiah 4:14 "Don't be afraid of them. Remember the Lord, who is great and awesome, and fight for your brothers, your sons and your daughters, your wives and your homes."

From that point forward, they realized they would have to be prepared to fight and work at the same time. As we commit ourselves to something noble, like sharing the Gospel, or counseling marriages, or fighting the scourge of abortion, we will need to remain prepared to fight the spiritual battle of discouragement and exhaustion at all times. Our enemy is real and "seeking someone to devour."

> *Nehemiah 4:16–18 From that day on, half of my men did the work, while the other half were equipped with spears, shields, bows and armor. The officers posted themselves behind all the people of Judah who were building the wall. Those who carried materials did their work with one hand and held a weapon in the other, and each of the builders wore his sword at his side as he worked.*

As builders of the wall, we need to keep the Sword of the Spirit—the Word of God—at our side at all times.

Tempered Victory

> *Nehemaih 6:15–16 So the wall was completed on the twenty-fifth of Elul, in fifty-two days. When all our enemies heard about this, all the surrounding nations were afraid and lost their self-confidence, because they realized that this work had been done with the help of our God.*

Ultimately, if God's people will commit themselves to diligently rebuilding the wall of righteousness, by which our nation was initially protected, I believe we will start to see hope flourish again, as we did at the founding of this blest land. Yes, there were holes of injustice in the wall even back then, but holy men and women have always risen up to fight these scourges. To this day, we continue to rebuild some of these sections of the wall.

Both Patrick Henry and Nehemiah fervently believed that the land God had given them was sacred—a holy land, set apart for freedom and righteousness. It was more than just a claim to a particular piece of property; it was a matter of protecting something God intended to be a lasting monument to His faithfulness. For Nehemiah, the elation of victory when the wall was completed had to be tempered with the fact that the wall would not have needed to be rebuilt if the Israelites had not turned their backs on God in the first place.

Our current state of affairs more closely mirrors Nehemiah's than Patrick Henry's. We are a nation that has turned its back on our Creator, and our walls are broken down. Spiritually we are enslaved to sin and complacency and comfort, and the walls have been reduced to rubble.

The Good News . . .

As I have said throughout this chapter, for every pivotal point in history there is a corresponding remnant God has set aside to carry on the faith. I believe the present-day remnant is in far better shape in terms of numbers than in times past. But even if only one percent of Christians lived passionately for the Lord, we would change the face of the earth.

Your Section of the Wall

There is one more interesting point I'd like to make about the story of Nehemiah. Scripture is very detailed in its account of which particular households worked on the different sections of the wall, even to the point of emphasizing when one man's family gave a more "zealous" effort than the others.

> *Neh. 3:20 " . . . Baruch son of Zabbai zealously repaired another section, from the angle to the entrance of the house of Eliaship the high priest."*

I point this out because every Christian has been given a section of the wall to repair, and our spiritual heritage is linked to how zealously we go about the work. I certainly don't want the records of Christian history to say, "The Tedesco family was given the such-and-such section of the wall, but they didn't get too far with it—although they did get real good at watching movies and playing video games."

I don't believe modern Christians agree with the idea that God has a very specific plan for each one of our lives—for which we were uniquely created—but everything in Scripture seems to reveal the exacting nature of God. I believe He does have a predetermined ideal for each one of us and our families, including where we should live and worship and serve.

> *Acts 17: 26 ". . . he determined the times set for them and the* ***exact places*** *where they should live." (emphasis added)*

Don't arrive singed.

The ultimate question is this: What will history say about us? In this chapter, we have examined the lives of Nehemiah and Patrick Henry. Both men left behind legacies that will continue to be studied until the end of time. Similarly, each one of us will leave behind a legacy whether we like it or not; will it be something we want mentioned in our eulogy? What is the legacy we will build on the foundation of Christ and the salvation freely given to us by His grace?

> *1 Corinthians 3:11–15 "For no one can lay any foundation other than the one already laid, which is Jesus Christ. If any man builds on this foundation using gold, silver, costly stones, hay or straw, his work will be shown for what it is, because the Day will bring it to light. It will be revealed with fire, and the fire will test the quality of each man's work. If what he has built survives, he will receive his reward. If it is burned up, he will suffer loss; he himself will be saved,* ***but only as one escaping through flames.****" (emphasis added)*

I want to arrive in heaven with a blaze of glory—without the stench of a burnt legacy.

Isaiah 28:5 "In that day the Lord Almighty will be a glorious crown, a beautiful wreath for the remnant of his people."

SECOND INTERMISSION
"embracing autumn"

Next to my house is an enormous maple tree, which every year during autumn puts on a breathtaking display of color, and this year was no different. I guess I should back up and explain that autumn has always been my favorite season, because it brings us face to face with one element of God's glory. Even though His glory is all around us, autumn holds the mystique of being a quick burst, and then it is gone. I imagine if the leaves were splendid colors year-round, we would not appreciate them nearly as much. Who knows? Maybe if they were orange and red all year and then suddenly turned green in the fall, we would drive around looking at green leaves.

Anyway, getting back to the story, as the final leaves were falling from this maple, my kids were busy amassing a large pile of them for the obvious purpose of wanting to please me by raking up the yard. Oops, back up again—one more detail. I have an annual ritual I share with my kids, during which I wait until most of the yard has been raked, and then I come out and promise to complete the work, as long as they promise not to jump into the pile. Once I finish, I turn my back, pretending to take a break while wiping my brow, and they sneak in behind me, jumping in and making a mess of the whole thing. (The rolling of my teenage son's eyes tells me they may be catching on to the fact that I don't really expect them not to jump in the leaves.) So I pretend to get angry, and we continue this ritual until someone inadvertently gets poked in the eye with a stick or a rake. Then we surrender the leaves to the evil leaf-sucker from the borough, and we put away the rakes for one more season.

Well, this year things worked out a little differently. I came out of the house for the annual ritual but was greeted by incredibly gusty winds. I looked across the yard and saw my youngest son, Sam, holding a sheet flapping in the wind as he was trying to save the leaves, but they were blowing everywhere, and he was becoming very upset. Meanwhile, my youngest daughter, Christa, was joyfully running through airborne debris, as the powerful gusts made mini tornadoes out of the leaves and dirt. She was having the time of her life getting pelted in the face, so I joined her.

After a short time of embarrassing myself in full view of the neighbors, I realized my son was still engaged in his futile effort to save the pile of leaves, and he was becoming increasingly more frustrated. So I took his face in my hands and said, "Sam, you've got to seize the moment! You're missing out on all the fun! All these leaves will be gone in a day or two, and you'll have missed out your last chance to enjoy them."

I then took a moment to explain how this experience was just like life, but he wasn't buying it, so I told him to grab a few more sheets, and I proceeded to help him try to save the leaves. Eventually, we gave up the fight and started jumping in the leaves, and shortly thereafter we were joined by the bunny, the dog and my other two kids, Josh and Karine. (I took plenty of pictures, which will probably remain on a disk somewhere for the next ten years until I have a need to embarrass one of my kids in front of his or her fiancé.)

It was one of those moments you wish would last forever, but like life, with the gusty winds came a heavy downpour. We quickly grabbed a few handfuls of leaves and carried them onto the front porch, and just like that, leaf-jumping season was over . . . but we enjoyed watching the powerful storm from the porch.

In so many ways, autumn really does represent life. Those of us who still consider ourselves to be young (which would be anyone my age or younger) tend to assume that we are in the springtime of our lives, living in denial of the fact that autumn will eventually arrive.

Then as the leaves begin to take on a white-ish gray-like appearance—and even start to fall—reality starts to set in. We have a choice; we can either grab a sheet in an effort to try to save the leaves, or we can embrace the autumn for what it is and live for the new life promised to us. And, just like spring, this new life is only possible once the old life passes away.

Some of us may not get the chance to embrace the final moments of life. Growing up, we had a tree in our yard that would dump most of its leaves in one night; no fanfare, no "Ooh!" and "Ahh!" One day the leaves would seem to be nice and healthy, and the next, they were gone.

Only God knows the number of our days, but any way you look at it, the leaves must fall to make way for the new life, and in our case, the new life is eternal. It makes no sense to curse the wind for blowing the leaves away, or even to curse the storm for shortening our enjoyment of the leaves. We need to embrace the autumn—embrace life.

> *Psalm 139:16–17 All the days ordained for me were written in your book before one of them came to be. How precious to me are your thoughts, O God! How vast is the sum of them!*

For the Christian, embracing life means far more than just appreciating God's blessings while you have them; it means realizing that everything worth embracing comes at a tremendous sacrifice. We are able to embrace life because death and pain and suffering have been swallowed up by the victory of the Cross.

> *Revelation 21:3–4 And I heard a loud voice from the throne saying, "Now the dwelling of God is with men, and he will live with them. They will be his people, and God himself will be with them and be their God. He will wipe every tear from their eyes. There will be no more death or mourning or crying or pain, for the old order of things has passed away."*

With gratitude, we embrace life by devoting every fiber of our beings to serving Christ. This is our legacy, and interestingly enough, this is the focus of the final section of this book.

PART III
leaving a legacy

CHAPTER 12
the legacy of relationships

The Mortar

The Three Components of a Legacy

Up to this point, I've spoken in abstract terms about leaving a legacy, but now I would like to take a look at how to apply all of this in real life. To leave a genuine legacy, the goal must not be the legacy; it must be serving and obeying God and letting *Him* establish the legacy. But this takes difficult, everyday decisions, not abstract contemplation. If this makes any sense, leaving a legacy is intentional, but it cannot become the goal. Put another way, Christian service and works, done for the purpose of having people hold you in high esteem when you are gone, will be consumed by flames in the end. We are to zealously rebuild our section of the wall because the Lord has asked it of us, not because our pride was hurt by the Babylonians who knocked it down.

The next three chapters will examine the Christian legacy in three different components: The Legacy of Relationships, The Legacy of Stewardship, and The Legacy of the Spirit. It is my hope that this section of the book will contain practical information for the construction of your section of the wall—the legacy you will leave behind.

Crumbling Mortar

The point I was making toward the end of chapter eleven was that if each one of us would set about taking responsibility for the section of the wall entrusted to us, a wall of righteousness would begin to rise from the ashes, reversing America's slide toward relativism and secularism.

The problem with this idealistic approach is that the crumbling relationships in our lives often make the building process futile. In a way, if our spiritual legacy can be represented by our section of the wall—which we are building to honor God—then the relationships in our lives are like the mortar that holds all the "precious stones" together.

For example, if I was a gifted pastor and had all the natural abilities to grow a mega-church of thousands, yet had a secret relationship on the side, my legacy would eventually crumble. No matter how impressive my life appears on the outside, if I have sinful or broken relationships undermining the structure, the enemy will eventually bring the whole wall tumbling down. Anyone who has owned a house with an old chimney knows it doesn't matter that high-quality bricks were used to build the chimney if the mortar between the bricks is crumbling.

A Would-be Legacy

Not too long ago I was driving through a cozy little neighborhood, and I was intrigued by what I observed on the front of every home in the plan; white crosses had been built into each home's masonry work. The neighborhood was probably built in the seventies and is currently being used as rental property, but it was obvious that it was originally intended to be something greater. So curiosity got the best of me and I stopped an elderly woman who looked as if she would know the history of the housing plan. As it turned out, she had only been there for two months, but she did know the history, and she filled me in on the sad details.

Now, you didn't hear this from me, but in her reluctance to want to share any of the juicy morsels of information, she let it slip that apparently the man who had developed the neighborhood was the would-be pastor of a small church. The congregation had dreams of using the main house as their meeting place, but before the master plan could be realized, the pastor became involved in an adulterous affair, and his legacy became rental property. The saddest part of the story was that the man had just passed away, and God only knows if he abandoned his faith altogether or if he arrived in heaven as "one escaping through the flames."

This was a man who obviously had a vision, but his inability to control his physical passions probably destroyed many relationships and brought his legacy tumbling to the ground.

The Clanging Cymbal

There is no good way to truly fathom how crucial the mortar of relationships is to the structural integrity of our life's work, but if we could, I believe we would make it the highest priority. It doesn't take an adulterous affair to destroy the work of our hands; sometimes it just takes selfishness or anger or simply a lack of communication. From my own limited experience, I honestly believe that if I see to it my children know without any doubt how much I love them, they will be able to see past my faults (within reason), and my life will still be a witness to them.

I've always liked the saying, "People don't care how much you know until they know how much you care." It sounds mushy, but it is supported by Scripture:

> *1 Corinthians 13:1–8 If I speak in the tongues of men and of angels, but have not love, I am only a resounding gong or a clanging cymbal. If I have the gift of prophecy and can fathom all mysteries and all knowledge, and if I have faith that can move mountains, but have not love, I am nothing. If I give all I possess to the poor and surrender my body to the flames, but have not love, I gain nothing.*
> *Love is patient, love is kind. It does not envy, it does not*

boast, it is not proud. It is not rude, it is not self-seeking, it is not easily angered, it keeps no record of wrongs. Love does not delight in evil but rejoices in the truth. It always protects, always trusts, always hopes, always perseveres. Love never fails.

If we were to truly live out this passage, we would see a profound difference in all of the relationships we share; marriages would be strengthened, families would pull together and the bonds between fellow Christians would be able to withstand the onslaught of the enemy.

More Muddy Waters

These three primary relationships—marriage, family and our relationships with fellow Christians—seem to be suffering greatly, as our society succumbs to moral relativism. Out of the three, I believe the marriage covenant is the most crucial to the spiritual survival of any culture, and consequently, it is under the greatest assault in ours. Even the Christian Church can't seem to agree on what the Biblical definition of marriage is. Just as an example, as I was writing this chapter, one of the mainline Christian denominations met to vote on whether or not to ordain homosexuals, adding even more confusion to this growing debate. One of the bewildering proposals was as follows: (This is an exact quote from an Associated Press article by Rachel Zoll)

> *"(One of the) measures would: Affirm the church ban on ordaining sexually active gays but allow bishops and church districts called synods to seek an exception for a particular candidate if that person is in a committed relationship and meets other conditions."*

In other words, "We're going to reaffirm our position that fornication and homosexuality are sins—unless the couple is really sincere about it—and then these are not sins, at least not really bad ones . . . we think. The Authority of the Church has spoken."

The vote took place, and astoundingly, nearly passed with a vote of 503–490. In other words, almost half of the leaders of the church (as in, people in charge, or shepherds of the flock, or those responsible for safeguarding the Holy Gospel) thought this proposal was a good idea. And who is to say that some of those who voted against it weren't holding out for an even more radical proposal?

If the leaders of the Christian Church continue to waver on such a fundamental issue as the sanctity of marriage, how can the Church speak with any authority on all the other issues of morality, virtue, and absolute truth? It is no wonder so many people enter marriage without any idea of how to make it work or what to do when adversity strikes.

A few paragraphs earlier, I introduced the idea that if we could somehow live out the message of 1 Corinthians 13, our relationships would be profoundly changed. But there is a much deeper issue at the very core of our beings upon which the success of such an idealistic goal hinges—the value of life. If the institution of marriage—the foundational relationship that holds every society together—is to be saved, and if family relationships are to be mended, and if Christian relationships are to be strengthened, it will all start with understanding the intrinsic value of each and every human life.

In His Image

Genesis 1:27 So God created man in his own image, in the image of God he created him; male and female he created them.

The whole concept of being created by God in His image is far beyond my ability to comprehend. How can something so finite and flawed bear any resemblance to my Creator? Yet there it is. So many things about the Christian faith fit this profile: "How can it be? . . . Yet there it is."

Ecclesiastes 11:5 As you do not know the path of the wind, or how the body is formed in a mother's womb, so you cannot understand the work of God, the maker of all things.

I take great comfort in the realization that I don't worship a God who can be contained or understood by the minds of those He created. It has taken scientists thousands of years (or millions depending on your denomination or school) to begin to understand the building blocks of life and how it was created, so it is not such a leap for me to have faith in God, my Creator.

A Butterfly Observed

I quoted the Scripture about being created "in His image" because if we can somehow comprehend the value placed on every life by God himself, we will begin to view all of our relationships in a whole new light.

Say, for example, I go to visit a butterfly conservatory and one of the volunteers takes me aside to excitedly point out a rare species of which only ten or eleven are known to exist in the world. Fascinated, I take out my camera and take several pictures, and then I take off my shoe and squash it. Through tears, the stunned volunteer asks, "Why . . . why . . . how could you do that?" In response I say to him, "Not to worry. I got the pictures I wanted."

In the same way, when we treat life or relationships with selfish disregard, or in the case of marriage, we discount the importance of it altogether, we commit a far more loathsome act. What is it that allows us to squash a spider but to hold in such high regard a butterfly or a hummingbird? It is the value we place on it, either because of its beauty or rarity or, in the case of the spider, the lack of safety we will feel when it makes its way into our beds.

But it is a grave sin to start assigning value to human life in the same way. For example, when a woman becomes pregnant, there are many tests made available to determine the health of the baby in order to give her "options," just in case the baby has Down's syndrome or some other abnormality. When I discovered what these tests were for, I was dumbfounded that the same physicians who daily experience the magnificence of life could treat it with such disdain.

Every day, mothers and fathers around the world are being asked to decide whether their child is a butterfly or a spider; in this way, we are assigning value to life based on its health, its beauty, its size, its convenience, its sex, its age, or even its usefulness. There is even a segment of our society that believes new parents should be given a grace period once their child is born to determine whether or not their child is a "wanted child." Fortunately, for now, it is still illegal to dispose of your child once it has been born—completely. Although where partial-birth abortion is still legal, a baby can be killed as long as its head is still partially within the mother—you know, to keep it from becoming human. And then we pray, "God Bless America."

Wonderfully Made

For reasons we will not understand until the end of days, God has made *humans* His crowning achievement; and even more perplexing, He has chosen to populate the heavens with the likes of us. We have been created for His glory, and regardless of what we think of ourselves or what sinful tendencies we regularly struggle with, He chose to breathe a soul into our unformed bodies at the moment of conception, giving us this incredible trust—the gift of life.

> *Psalm 139:13–17 For you created my inmost being, you knit me together in my mother's womb.* **I praise you because I am fearfully and wonderfully made**; *your works are wonderful, I know that full well. My frame was not hidden from you when I was made in the secret place. When I was woven together in the depths of the earth, your eyes saw my unformed body. All the days ordained for me were written in your book before one of them came to be. How precious to me are your thoughts, O God! How vast is the sum of them! (emphasis added)*

The first time I can remember truly gaining an appreciation for life was at the birth of my first child, Joshua. I recall being awestruck that an actual little human being had just emerged from my wife; I was also amazed that anything could make it through such a traumatic experience and live. There is nothing that compares to watching the births of each of my four children; these were experiences no book could have prepared me for. For the first time I could see past the natural beauty of my wife and recognize that her whole being had been "fearfully and wonderfully made," and for some reason God had entrusted her life and the lives of these four children to *me*.

If we learn to cherish God's creation, especially the creation of human life, we may then humbly ask for God's sovereign hand to intervene in our struggling marriages and our broken homes and our fractured churches, and I believe we will experience his healing power.

The Rub

It is virtually impossible to maintain a continuous awareness of the value God has placed on all life, especially when that precious-creation-of-a-spouse has just stormed out of the house after berating you with a long, verbal lashing of insults. I can almost hear the voice of the single mother out there saying, "Why don't you bring a helping of your neat little theology over to my house at two in the morning and feed it to my kid so I can get some sleep for a change?" And there's the rub.

Each time I have gotten that rare glimpse into the magnificence of life, a healthy dose of reality has quickly swooped down and snatched it away. So, I am not suggesting we live by the emotional awareness of the splendor of creation. What I am suggesting is that when we acknowledge this splendor before God through the decisions we make, both individually and as a nation, God pours out His grace, making it truly possible to live out the passage on "love" from 1 Corinthians. There is no better place to start—that is, with the grace of God—as we begin to repair these relationships, assuring that our legacies will withstand the test of time and adversity.

The Plight of Humanity

Many people may not realize this, but the "Love Chapter" is not an excerpt from a sermon delivered at a wedding; nor was it premarital counseling given to a starry-eyed, engaged couple. It is taken from a letter of reprimand written by the Apostle Paul to the Christian church at Corinth. The church was in great turmoil because of the immorality within the congregation and because of the factions being established by the believers; members of the church were dividing into separate camps behind their favorite apostles, and Paul scolds them for it:

> *1 Corinthians 3:3–4 "You are still worldly. For since there is jealousy and quarreling among you, are you not worldly? Are you not acting like mere men? For when one says, 'I follow Paul,' and another, 'I follow Apollos,' are you not mere men?"*

Paul begins his chapter on "love" by pointing out that the spiritual gifts are useless without love. He does this because there were power struggles going on within the church, as many of the believers found themselves comparing spiritual gifts. One person might have said something like, "I've got the gift of tongues." And another would respond with, "Oh yeah? Well I've got the gift of prophecy, and Paul says prophecy trumps the gift of tongues every time." As a result, when they met together to celebrate the Lord's Supper, it was a spiritually fruitless pursuit, and Paul addresses this problem with a hint of sarcasm:

> *1 Corinthians 11:17–19 "In the following directives I have no praise for you, for your meetings do more harm than good. In the first place, I hear that when you come together as a church, there are divisions among you, and to some extent I believe it. No doubt there have to be differences among you to show which of you have God's approval."*

The cynic in me gets a little bit of pleasure from the fact that people were just as selfish and petty in the early Church as we are now. And this is partly the reason I point these things out; we belong to the human race, and from the beginning of time humans have tended to act like people—selfish, prideful, jealous and unforgiving.

Let's face it. Our human nature derives more momentary pleasure from gossip and jealousy than it does from Christian love and unity. It is the same in marriage; we would rather sleep on the couch and revel in the victory of being right than reconcile and grow closer to each other. And in family relationships, we would rather spend the next thirty years letting that parent or child or sibling know just how deep the scars are from the pain they inflicted on us, than to experience the healing power of forgiveness.

The Hope of Humanity

The other half of the story is more encouraging. Because we are no different now than the Christians in Paul's day, the teaching and advice offered for relationships through his letter is just as relevant now as it ever was. The scope of just this one chapter on love is astounding, and the fact that it is used so frequently at weddings shows that the principles for dealing with relationships within the Church are no different than those for husband and wife, or for family.

As I attempt to address the difficult subject of *relationships*, I would like to avoid sounding like a contemporary philosopher by saying things like, "Can't we all just get along?" Any counselor will tell you that relationships are quite complex, and there are never any quick fixes that work across the board. I realize anything I write needs to be just as true for the man or woman whose spouse has had an affair as it is for the couple arguing over finances. It must be equally true for the church fractured by a pastor's secret past as it is for those fighting over the location of the organ. And it must also be equally true for the man or woman who was sexually abused as a child by a close relative or family acquaintance as it is for two siblings feuding over whose child took the first swing.

So rather than try to empathize and totally miss the mark, I'll try not to stray too far from the principles in the Apostle Paul's commentary on love and how they apply to relationships.

Repairing the Mortar

At the beginning of this chapter, I likened relationships to the joints of mortar holding together the legacy we are building. Sometimes it seems as if there are people in our lives who make it their primary mission to chisel away the mortar every chance they get. Who knows? Maybe each one of us plays that role in someone else's life. I know it *seems* like it is always the other person doing the chiseling, but entertain the idea for just a moment that it takes two people to effectively remove the mortar—one to hold the chisel and one to swing the hammer. In addition, let's say the hammer represents selfishness and the chisel is an unforgiving heart. The one swinging the hammer of selfishness is the one actually committing the offense, but the one holding on to the chisel of the unforgiving heart makes it possible for the hammer to be the most effective. Sometimes in marriage we even take turns holding each other's chisels to give our spouse a chance to swing.

The only way to counteract this abusive cycle is to focus on the two principles that effectively pry the hammer and chisel from our hands.

> *1 Corinthians 13:4–5* "Love . . . is not self-seeking . . ." (the hammer)
> "Love . . . keeps no record of wrongs." (the chisel)

These two principles alone hold the secrets to healing marriages, mending families and unifying churches, and most significantly, they embody the life and the crucifixion of Christ—love in human form.

"It's all about me."

One of the most glaring characteristics of the American culture is the glorification of "self," or narcissism. This is one significant reason people around the world are so hostile toward us and why we are considered the "Ugly Americans." Retailers even promote after-Christmas "It's all about me" sales for those who didn't receive exactly what they wanted in order to adequately celebrate Christ's birth. But I don't wish to bash Americans for enjoying the wealth and prosperity resulting from a free, capitalistic society. After all, wealth allows us to aid those impoverished nations around the world when tragedy strikes, and wealth also makes Christian missionary work possible. I simply wish to point out the ultimate effect of the constant barrage of subliminal (and not-so-subliminal) messages that say, "You are the center of the universe . . . You deserve to have everything you have ever desired . . . It's all about you . . . Your friends will worship you if you buy this 85" HypnoPlasmaTronic Brain-softening Home Theatre."

This atmosphere of "self" makes the whole principle from 1 Corinthians—"Love is not self-seeking"—seem quite foreign. But when you stop to contemplate it, most of the pain and difficulty we experience—or that we cause others to experience—results from acts of selfishness. Our human nature insists on having its desires met, even if it is at the expense of others. It could be a perverted desire for sex, power, money or vengeance, or it might just be the result of a character flaw, like selfishly meeting the needs of an addiction at the expense of family and friends.

> *Philippians 2:3 Do nothing out of selfish ambition or vain conceit, but in humility consider others better than yourselves. Each of you should look not only to your own interests, but also the interests of others.*

It all boils down to this—"Love is not self-seeking." The most genuine expression of love, then, is not primarily displays of affection, but it is forfeiting our right to satisfy the "self;" in other words, it is self-sacrifice. The most basic human instinct or desire above all else is self-preservation, so then the supreme act of love is to give one's life for another.

> *John 15:12–13 "My command is this: Love each other as I have loved you. Greater love has no one than this, that he lay down his life for his friends."*

The vast majority of us will never be asked to literally give our lives for another, but we can still honor the intrinsic value of those God has entrusted to us by laying down our lives in practical ways. For the husband and father, it might be something as simple as temporarily setting aside a favorite hobby or pastime in order to assist your wife in retrieving her sanity from the diaper pail. For the wife, it might mean resisting the urge to knock your husband down a peg or two, even though you have sufficient ammunition to do so. For the writer, it could mean thinking twice before dumping your coffee on the lap of that self-important salesman who has moved his home office to the table next to you and thinks everyone within a three block radius would like to hear the details of his business transactions. But for everyone, it entails living with one another's faults, recognizing our own, and praying for the grace to be able to change our selfish ways.

Many people will be asked to make great sacrifices for each other. My nephew has suffered through cancer treatments twice, so my sister has been in contact with many families of cancer patients. She has seen the effects of this traumatic experience either destroy families or unify them, and she says it is usually obvious early on which families will survive; it is typically the ones who are not bitter toward each other and realize the need to make sacrifices. When life throws us a curve, we very quickly find out how selfish we really are.

Prying Away the Hammer

As each one of us learns to put the needs of others above our own, our grip on the hammer of selfishness begins to loosen, and eventually we see the wisdom of laying it down altogether. As my wife and I have learned to relinquish our right to cling to selfish desires or preconceived notions about what life owes us, we have seen drastic changes in the way we relate to each other. And if I had to single out one change that has been more unifying than any other, it would be our willingness to surrender the "record of wrongs" we had been so diligently keeping.

For the first several years of our marriage, each time we would argue we would retrieve our mental lists of betrayals and failures and use them as ammunition to win the argument. But we soon found out that it was pointless to hold the chisel if no one was swinging the hammer; it is impossible to be sel*fless* and unforgiving at the same time. So I would have to say, it is the willingness to forgive—to surrender this "record of wrongs"—that is at the heart of every strong relationship. No matter how good our intentions, we will never be able to remove every last bit of "self" from our hearts, but if we are at least willing to forgive, repairing the mortar of relationships will prove to be a far more achievable goal.

The Heart of Forgiveness

This is where it gets difficult. More often than not, when there is a desire for forgiveness and healing, it is extremely one-sided, and the other side is usually unwilling or unable to take part. Adding to this difficulty, there are times when the nature of the offense is so heinous that the human heart is incapable of bridging the gap between the desire for forgiveness and the ability to offer it. Given these conditions, we have to conclude that true forgiveness must not *require* both parties to participate, and it must not require the assurance that the offense will never again be committed. Most importantly, it must depend on a supernatural grace and not the ability of the human heart to manufacture a feeling of affection toward the offender.

For those who have been deeply wounded but genuinely desire to be healed through forgiveness and don't know where to start, all

I can offer is the example of the Cross. As Jesus was being crucified he prayed, "Father, forgive them, for they do not know what they are doing." (Luke 23:34) He had every right to be angry and resentful and could have said something more like, "Father, punish these wicked men tenfold for what they have done to me." But He didn't; He said, "Father, forgive them . . ." Not only were they not asking for forgiveness, but they were nailing His hands and His feet to the cross. He was able to pray this prayer because He knew His sacrifice would provide the way for forgiveness of all sins, including ours.

The Economy of Forgiveness

In the "Parable of the Unmerciful Servant," Jesus tells the story of a king who wished to settle his accounts with those who owed him money. One of his servants owed him a large sum and could not pay, so when the servant begged for more time to settle the debt, the king had mercy on him and cancelled the debt altogether. Later on, that same man found a fellow servant who owed him just a tiny fraction of the amount the king had just cancelled for him, but he choked his fellow servant and demanded payment. When the poor man begged for more time, he refused and had him thrown in jail. As you probably already know, the king found out what the unmerciful servant did and became angry, throwing him in jail to be tortured until he could pay back all he owed.

By telling this parable (knowing He would soon suffer the cross and cancel the debts of all of us), Jesus was establishing both the key to forgiveness and the requirement of forgiveness. First, the Cross is the key to forgiveness because if we could just realize the enormous cost of our own forgiveness—the torture and death of the innocent Son of God—it would lessen our need for payment from the one who has become indebted to us. Second, the Cross established the requirement of forgiveness, because if we are willing to accept the forgiveness offered through Christ, we must then be willing to offer that same forgiveness to others.

As We Forgive Those

Every Christian has prayed *The Lord's Prayer*, and many of us pray it at least once per week. But if we took the time to study each line, I believe we would think twice before praying the words, "Forgive us our trespasses, as we forgive those who trespass against us." This is the only line Jesus takes the time to clarify after finishing the prayer. He says:

> *Matthew 6:14–15 "For if you forgive men when they sin against you, your heavenly Father will also forgive you. But if you do not forgive men their sins, your Father will not forgive your sins."*

In this passage, Jesus is not spitefully saying, "If the Father is going to forgive you, the least you could do for Him is forgive others." A crucial element of receiving Christ's forgiveness is repentance, and true repentance means letting go of all sins, including the unwillingness to forgive. He is also quite aware that this particular sin is at the root of most vengeance, bitterness, anger and rage; these things destroy marriages, wreck family relationships, and divide churches, and it is impossible to live a life pleasing to the Lord with these things in your heart.

> *Ephesians 4:30–32 "And do not grieve the Holy Spirit of God, with whom you were sealed for the day of redemption. Get rid of all bitterness, rage and anger, brawling and slander, along with every form of malice. Be kind and compassionate to one another, **forgiving each other, just as in Christ God forgave you.**" (emphasis added)*

At the very heart of Jesus' mission on earth was to provide the way for the forgiveness of sins; consequently, you can be sure Satan's primary goal for marriages, families and churches is to divide and outwit us by breeding division and resentment:

> *2 Corinthians 2:10–11 "I have forgiven in the sight of Christ*

for your sake, in order that Satan might not outwit us. For we are not unaware of his schemes."

Out of all the things Jesus asked of His apostles through his teaching, the issue of forgiveness was the one that provoked the most animated response:

Luke 17:3–4 "If your brother sins, rebuke him, and if he repents forgive him. If he sins against you seven times in a day, and seven times comes back to you and says, 'I repent,' forgive him." The apostles said to the Lord, "Increase our faith!"

The phrase "Increase our faith!" from my NIV translation does not adequately capture the essence of the original Greek. I think a more accurate translation would be, "Yeah, right—not in this lifetime!"

Forgiveness Defined

If I had to reduce the definition of forgiveness to one sentence, I would say, "Forgiveness is surrendering your right to inflict pain or guilt as retribution for an offense, while also surrendering your right to cling to bitterness and resentment, no matter how justified it may be." As the apostles said, "Increase our faith!"

Inevitably, the question arises, "I guess I should be a doormat, then?" So just to clarify the issue, sometimes Christian love requires difficult decisions—or "tough love"—that ultimately result in pain and sacrifice for both sides of the relationship, but righteousness, not vengeance, needs to be at the heart of these decisions. Furthermore, in serious or criminal cases, forgiveness does not release the other person from the obligation of making amends before God or the legal system; justice is a crucial element in the Scriptures and in our society, and without it there would be chaos. In short, forgiveness is not characterized by inaction, but by a purity of motive.

Within the doctrines of Christianity, the principle of forgiveness is without question one of the most difficult to abide by, mostly because the hurt and pain and emotion are real, and the natural response to these is the desire to inflict punishment on anybody and everybody involved. But it is important to understand that offering forgiveness does not mean it is your responsibility to heal the wounds; it is simply a way of saying, "Lord, my heart is now yours, and only You are able to mend this relationship and make it whole." In some ways, the "forgiving" is our job, but the "forgetting" is left up to the work of Christ.

I said earlier that true forgiveness must not depend on the other person being ready or willing, or even still alive, because it is the Lord who bridges the gaps in our relationships with His Cross. The Cross of Christ spans the chasms between time, space, eternity, and relationships, and in its purest form, *forgiveness is the Cross*. Consequently, to bring this chapter full-circle, understanding forgiveness means understanding the Cross. At the heart of the Cross is God's unconditional love for us—not because of any virtue or piety on our part, but because of the intrinsic value of each and every human being conceived in his or her mother's womb.

John 3:16 "For God so loved the world that he gave his one and only Son . . ."

I wholeheartedly believe that if we are to experience God's healing hand in our relationships—the mortar that holds together our churches, our families, and our nation—it will start with gaining a true appreciation and respect for the God-ordained value of life. I would like to devote the final section of this chapter to one more human effort to put this idea of "intrinsic value" into words.

Old Barns

As a writer, I have determined that it is not only preferable but quite necessary to indulge certain eccentricities as a way of lending credibility to my writing. I sometimes imagine spending my waning years wandering the countryside in a bathrobe, smoking an unlit pipe, and occasionally spouting poetry for no apparent reason.

With that in mind, admitting I have a fascination with old barns seems perfectly sensible, and having spent a fair amount of time on the country roads of Ohio, I've seen my fair share of them. The fascination is partly due to the history of the barn and partly because some of them seem to defy the laws of physics in their ability to remain standing, with half of their foundations crumbled away. Frank Lloyd Wright would have had a difficult time designing such a cantilevered barn without it falling over. There is nothing that compares to standing inside of a 120 year-old barn and wondering, "Is this the day it finally collapses?"

Laws of physics aside, pondering the history of an old barn holds more fascination for me than the fact that it is still standing; just to see the hand-hewn beams and imagine the work that went into constructing it is something in itself. You can't help but ponder all the hours in the field of the farmer and his family who built the barn. From there, you wonder if he had sons who continued the farming tradition, or if they considered it a curse. Was it all toil, or were there times of enjoyment and laughter within the barn? Were there children who spent hours playing hide-and-seek in the loft, or were their childhood years stolen from them by anger or bitterness or necessity? Was the barn built by a husband and wife living their dream of living off the land, or was this dream cut short by disease or tragedy?

Every barn almost seems to have a soul made up of all the dreams and memories and successes and failures—the moments of pain hopefully offset by the moments of joy. Even when standing in a dilapidated, run-down, old barn, in which the sky is readily viewed through the roof rafters, there is an awesome realization that there is probably over a hundred years of history wrapped up in its walls. Some barns have been remarkably maintained over the years, and some look as if they were painted once and never touched again, but all have a history. Some stand as proud monuments to years of meticulous care-taking, while others tell a story marked by years of neglect.

I am learning to realize that if old barns are able to hold such fascination and mystique for me, how much more should the people in my life? How much more magnificent is the creation of a human life than the construction of an old barn? How much more intriguing is the history and personality of my wife, or children, or parents than the history of a neglected barn? Furthermore, how will my life permanently affect these intriguing personalities entrusted to me?

In a very limited sense, each one of us resembles an old barn in the making; each one of us is stamped with a certain personality by our Creator, and our life circumstances are in many ways chosen for us, much like the location of a barn. But like the soul of a barn, this incredible gift of life is indelibly stamped—either for good or for bad—by the relationships we choose and those chosen for us by God or by circumstance. Just as the love or neglect by a parent leaves a permanent legacy within each one of us, we do the same for the relationships around us.

I am sure if you were to isolate one moment in the life of a barn, say, for example, tossing a bail of hay or cleaning up after an inconsiderate animal, it would not seem all that significant to the farmer—no more than changing a diaper would seem to the mother of a newborn. But I am sure even the farmer would be amazed if he were to see the whole history of the barn on a timeline.

Sometimes in order to get a proper perspective of the value God places on life, we need to step outside of the moment and try to grasp the big picture. Even if we just examine this one snapshot called our earthly life (compared to our eternal life), we would be bewildered at the vast array of experiences one life represents. Now compare this with the eternal value of a soul spent in perfect union with the heavenly Father and the unfathomable mysteries of our existence unveiled before our eyes, and only then will we have a starting place to help unlock the treasure of the Cross.

Once again, the key to our Legacy of Relationships—and to the selfless love and forgiveness these relationships require—is hidden in the message of the Cross and in what that message tells us about the intrinsic value of every human life. This fundamental truth needs to be at the core of the decisions we make, individually, within the Church, and as a nation.

Every aspect of the Christian journey is wrapped up in the words of John 3:16, so I'd like to quote it again to end this chapter.

John 3:16 "For God so loved the world that he gave his one and only Son . . ."

CHAPTER 13
the legacy of stewardship

The Costly Stones

Psalm 49:10–11, 16–17 For all can see that wise men die; the foolish and senseless alike perish and leave their wealth to others. Their tombs will remain their houses forever, their dwellings for endless generations, though they had named lands after themselves . . . Do not be overawed when a man grows rich, when the splendor of his house increases; for he will take nothing with him when he dies . . .

For those who will read these verses and with a groan say, "Oh great. He is going to play the 'class-warfare' card," or for those who might be enthusiastically thinking, "Good. He's going to nail the rich," this chapter will satisfy neither. As a matter of fact, I need to carefully word what I say, just in case the Lord calls me to evangelize the wealthy. He may need to bless me with a vacation home in the Outer Banks so that I am better equipped to relate to their struggles, and I must be willing to shoulder that burden.

The fact is—beautiful homes and architecture have always been a weakness of mine, so I need to regularly come back to these verses to help maintain an eternal perspective.

Surprised by Death

The sole purpose for starting this chapter with the verses pertaining to wealth and death is to introduce the relationship between stewardship and mortality, and to encourage an eternal perspective on how we use the earthly gifts God bestows on us. The problem with the issue of mortality is that the people most qualified to speak on the subject don't live to tell about it. Regardless of how many generations come and go before us, we tend to live as though death was something that happens to other people. But there have been many lengthy studies done on the issue of death, carried out by countless prestigious government agencies, and the findings have been remarkably consistent: "One out of every one people die." Yet we find ourselves surprised by death in the realization that we just spent our entire lives living for ourselves. In other words, we have expended our health, our energy, our wealth, our time and our gifts, talents, and abilities on fulfilling our own human desires.

So we continue, generation after generation, to devote our talents and our resources to the glorification of "self" at the expense of our families, our churches and our nation. There is a popular saying that I believe strikes at the very heart of the issue: "Nobody on their deathbed has ever said, 'I wish I would have spent more time at work.'" There is something about being near death in some way, either in possibility or in reality, which puts life into perspective. You could engrave your name on every building in New York City, but death trumps fame and fortune every time. Or you could be the best in the world at putting a little white ball into a slightly larger cup, but if you never learn to use that notoriety for an eternal purpose, death will sneak up on you like a tiger and shred your legacy to bits.

I mentioned earlier that each one of us is leaving a legacy whether we like it or not; this idea of the stewardship of our blessings plays a huge part in determining what that legacy will be. When the last trumpet sounds, this legacy will be tested by fire, and the quality of the materials used in its construction will be very quickly revealed. If our legacy is built out of earthly accomplishments, it will amount to having built our wall out of "hay or straw," but if we devote ourselves to serving God, the wall will be built out of "costly stones."

Scripture seems to speak about the topic of financial stewardship more than most others, so I'll expand on this area first, but I think you'll find that the general principles will apply to all areas of stewardship. Jesus taught that it was not possible to "serve both God and Money" (Mt. 6:24), and He told many parables addressing the issue. So I don't believe it is possible to overstate the need for a biblical approach as we wade into this touchy subject. Also, I consider myself a "work in progress" in terms of fully and completely surrendering this area of my life to Christ, so I'll try to let the authority of Scripture speak in place of anything that is lacking in my experience.

Stewardship of Finances

Moths and Rust

Why bother? Many people might ask what the point is to devoting our resources to the service of the kingdom of heaven; after all, "Who really cares if the wall of my legacy is a short, little, stubby pile of rubble when I die? Being saved is what really counts, right?" Well, there are many good self-serving reasons to care, so I'll begin with those. For starters, Scripture seems to tell us that there will be a system of heavenly rewards based on how we managed our earthly possessions.

> *Matthew 6:19–21, 24 "Do not store up for yourselves treasures on earth, where moth and rust destroy, and where thieves break in and steal. But store up for yourselves treasures in heaven, where moth and rust do not destroy, and where thieves do not break in and steal. For where your treasure is, there your heart will be also . . . You cannot serve both God and money."*

If our hearts are set on acquiring everything this world has to offer, we will forfeit the "treasures in heaven" promised in the Scripture above. Now, I don't know what form these heavenly treasures will take, but I know we serve a God who wishes to lavish the best on His people, and I am willing to bet it will be infinitely better than anything our minds can conceive. I once heard a quote that drives home this concept of storing up treasures in heaven: "He is no fool who forfeits that which he cannot keep for that which he cannot lose."

Another good self-serving, yet common sense reason for choosing God's approach to finances is the contentment and peace we experience from learning to be satisfied with what we have and holding on loosely to any financial blessing He brings our way. It is easy to shake our heads in disbelief when a rich entertainer expresses discontentment with life or even commits suicide. But their discontent should be a glaring testimony to those of us who wish to grab everything life has to offer: The acquisition of wealth, fame, fortune, and power rarely brings the contentment we expect, and in many cases, it brings just the opposite.

> *1 Timothy 6:6–10 "But Godliness with contentment is great gain. For we brought nothing into the world, and we can take nothing out of it. But if we have food and clothing, we will be content with that. People who want to get rich fall into temptation and a trap and into many foolish and harmful desires that plunge men into ruin and destruction. For the love of money is a root of all kinds of evil. Some people, eager for money, have wandered from the faith and pierced themselves with many griefs."*

To learn contentment is something rarely achieved in this life, but the verses above show us that one of the keys to unlocking this rare treasure is to keep from becoming enamored with the trappings of wealth. How many times have we heard about multi-million dollar lottery winners whose lives have been destroyed by the "harmful desires" fulfilled through the availability of cash? But again, most of us would be happy to take that chance. For us, it will be different (right?) because we're more level-headed.

Just to Clarify

To be sure, it is just as possible for someone making ten thousand dollars per year to have a sinful approach toward money as it is for the millionaire. For example, Scripture warns us against using debt to finance a lifestyle above our level of income.

> *Proverbs 22:26–27 Do not be a man who strikes hands in a pledge or puts up security for debts; if you lack the means to pay, your very bed will be snatched from under you.*

And believe it or not, laziness can be just as much of a sin as chasing wealth, especially if it involves not providing for your family.

> *1 Timothy 5:8 If anyone does not provide for his relatives, and especially his immediate family, he has denied the faith and is worse than an unbeliever.*

Even if a person is dirt-poor, sometimes the eagerness to get rich can cause a person to chase all kinds of schemes and fantasies instead of working diligently within the boundaries of God's provision. These fantasies might include using your last two dollars on the lottery or at the casino, or even investing in a shady, too-good-to-be-true, rags-to-riches scheme.

> *Proverbs 28:19–20 He who works his land will have abundant food, but the one who chases fantasies will have his fill of poverty. A faithful man will be richly blessed, but one eager to get rich will not go unpunished.*

So it is not the possession of money that is sinful, but the unhealthy pursuit and use of it.

The Deceitfulness of Wealth

Getting back to the question, "Why bother?" I labeled the first two reasons as "self-serving" not because they are evil or wrong, but because each of us will personally benefit from them, at least in regard to treasures in heaven and earthly contentment. But the ultimate selfish—yet perfectly valid—reason to do it God's way is the effect "the deceitfulness of wealth" can have on the eternal condition of our souls. In the Scripture quoted earlier from 1 Timothy, the Apostle Paul writes to Timothy, "Some people, eager for money, have wandered from the faith . . ." Now the first question you might ask could be, "How genuine is the conversion of someone who is able to be drawn away from the faith by money?" And this is a valid question, but I just want to point out that there are no wasted words in Scripture, and I believe there is more we are meant to glean from a verse like this.

In many parables, Jesus reveals a link between the "love of money" and our ability to be receptive to the Gospel. Returning to the "Parable of the Sower" explained in chapter three, you'll recall that in the account of the seed that fell among the thorns, the poor growing conditions resulted from an improper perspective on wealth:

> *Matthew 13:22 "The one who received the seed that fell among the thorns is the man who hears the word, but the worries of this life and the deceitfulness of wealth choke it, making it unfruitful."*

Wealth is "deceitful" in that it makes promises it can't keep—promises of happiness and contentment and bliss and marital harmony. But we have been uniquely designed by our Creator to have those desires met through our Savior, and I have yet to meet one person who can substantiate the claim that wealth is able to fulfill these desires and longings.

Wealth is also deceitful in its ability to create an imaginary wall around those who have it, causing them to trust in their riches instead of the provision of God. This results in a prideful self-sufficiency, which is the first step toward a person's eternal downfall.

> *Proverbs 18:11–12 The wealth of the rich is their fortified city; they imagine it an unscalable wall. Before his downfall a man's heart is proud, but humility comes before honor.*

The deceitfulness of wealth also causes us to envy our neighbor, and to "covet thy neighbor's goods."

> *Ecclesiastes 4:4 And I saw that all labor and all achievement spring from man's envy of his neighbor. This too is meaningless, a chasing after the wind.*

And finally, the deceitfulness of wealth keeps us from ever being satisfied, no matter how much money we have. The more we have, the more we want, and consequently, the less sleep we get because of the worries that accompany great riches.

> *Ecclesiastes 5:10–12 Whoever loves money never has enough; whoever loves wealth is never satisfied with his income. This too is meaningless. As goods increase, so do those who consume them. And what benefit are they to the owner except to feast his eyes on them? The sleep of the laborer is sweet, whether he eats little or much, but the abundance of a rich man permits him no sleep.*

A Modern Day Tragedy

As we allow ourselves to be deceived by the pursuit of wealth, very often our children become casualties as well. In preparation for this chapter, I read an article by Patricia Sellers from a 2003 edition of *Fortune* magazine entitled, "Gone With the Wind." The article sadly chronicles the life, the successes, and the failures of the billionaire Ted Turner, and it proves the devastating effect that a father's pursuit of self-worth through worldly achievement can have on a child—in this particular case, Ted Turner's father.

In the article, Turner laments the difficulties of being "down to his last billion," after having been worth more than ten billion at one point in his career. His imaginary, "unscalable wall" of billions had shrunk considerably, and between arrogant comments about his "Turnerverse," he expresses his "fear of abandonment" and "a feeling that he has lost control." Throughout the interview, it becomes quite evident that his father has done more than any other to shape his world view, and Ted's success has been driven by a desire to outdo him or to make him proud—I'm not sure which. In his mid-sixties at the time of the interview, his roller-coaster comments revealed a man who had come face to face with his mortality and didn't know where to turn.

But the most tragic part of the story is his father's advice to him—just before his father committed suicide. The legacy Ted's father dumped into his lap at the age of twenty-four came in the form of this advice: "You should set goals beyond your reach so you always have something to live for." How incredibly sad; judging by the content of the interview, Ted was continuing to pay the debt on that comment forty-plus years later. Instead of learning from his father about the bankruptcy of the soul that results from the pursuit of human dreams and wealth, he followed his father's advice and is trying to single-handedly conquer and/or save the universe. For someone who has accomplished so much and has been so successful, during the interview he sounded more like a child lost at an amusement park, just hoping a familiar hand would soon guide him home. It is a heart-breaking story, but it is one we desperately need to learn from.

When I heard Ted Turner's story, I thanked God I was fortunate enough to have the example of a father who chose to serve God's kingdom over pursuing what could have been a very comfortable career as a senior engineer. He is very brilliant in his field and would have been rewarded handsomely for his dedication to the company, but he chose the less financially rewarding field of Christian service. We weren't poor by anyone's standards, but we could have worn more socially acceptable brands of shoes. Anyway, I remember the example of my father having a profound impact on me, even at a young age, because it showed me his faith was real—real enough to translate into action.

So for those who are parents, everything we do reverberates for decades, and that legacy will shape the lives of our children and grandchildren long after we have departed this life. And for everyone, if God has blessed you with billions or just enough to get by, give thanks and devote it to the service of His kingdom, and you will store up for yourselves treasures in heaven.

Psalm 62:10 ". . . though your riches increase, do not set your heart on them."

Into Context

You may be wondering what the issue of financial stewardship has to do with the overall theme of this book, but I can assure you, it is a very crucial piece. I mentioned the self-serving reasons to be financially responsible first because they are the easiest to list and to verify with Scripture. But for those of us who count ourselves among the remnant, personal gain cannot be the driving force behind the decisions we make. We need to be driven by our desire to uphold the honor of Jesus Christ in our society, living by the conviction that we need to win this culture war in which we find ourselves engaged.

Nehemiah did not set about rebuilding the walls of Jerusalem because of the promise of heavenly rewards; he did it because of his passion for the glory and the honor of God, and restoring the walls of Jerusalem represented restoring God's promise to his people. By no means do I intend to imply that America is the "New Jerusalem," but in many ways, this beautiful land represents God's promise to those early settlers who were willing to sacrifice their lives to be able to worship freely. We need to be just as passionate as Nehemiah and our forefathers in our desire to turn our culture back toward the heart of God.

Like a military war, the culture war has costs associated with it, and if we intend to see change at the highest levels, it will come at a financial cost. As I mentioned earlier, the Revolutionary War could have easily ended prematurely in defeat, if it hadn't been for Robert Morris and his wealthy associates, who essentially financed the war. In much the same way, the effort to stop the slide of the branches of our government toward secularism will take tremendous amounts of prayer, human effort and money, and by being a faithful steward of our blessings, we put ourselves into a position to make a difference. For example, if poor decisions cause me to be saddled with tremendous amounts of debt, it is likely that the credit card companies will devour the portion of my budget that should be going toward the Church and to the service of God's kingdom.

The countless groups opposing the Church and its values are very well organized and tremendously diligent, so we need to be doubly so. For example, groups like Planned Parenthood and the ACLU exist almost exclusively to undermine the traditional family and to minimize the role of the Church in our society, and their members are passionate about funding those efforts. Even within the walls of the Church, there are well-funded groups seeking to undermine the traditional Judeo-Christian value system, so as Christians we need to be faithful in our tithing and shrewd in our charitable giving. I've already quoted the following verse, but it is worth repeating.

Matthew 10:16 "I am sending you out like sheep among the wolves. Therefore be shrewd as snakes and as innocent as doves."

Most of us don't consider ourselves activists, but this does not remove us from the responsibility to fight for righteousness and to support those on the front lines of the battles being fought for God's kingdom. In every society since the beginning of time, there have been great injustices visited upon whole classes and races of people, either through murder, slavery, abortion, religious persecution, etc., and each one of us will be held accountable for how we responded to the injustices of our particular time.

> *Proverbs 24:11–12 "Rescue those being led away to death; hold back those staggering toward slaughter. If you say, 'But we knew nothing about this,'* **does not he who weighs the heart perceive it?** *Does not he who guards your life know it? Will he not repay each person according to what he has done?"* (emphasis added)

This is why stewardship on every level—not just financial—is such a weighty issue. It is not about maximizing your potential as a talented or financially blest Christian; it is about obeying the voice of God and fighting for His kingdom. There is no higher calling.

The fundamental truth behind the concept of stewardship is this: Every thing we have, whether it is financial blessing, personal talents, health, time, relationships, etc., is on loan to us from God and can be taken away at any given moment. It is our obligation to devote it all to His glory.

Stewardship of Talents

In the Parable of the Talents, Jesus tells the story of a man going away on a trip, and before leaving, the man entrusted his money to his servants. To the first he gave five talents, to the second two, and to the last he gave one talent. When he returned to settle accounts with his servants, he found that two of them had invested the money and doubled it, but the last one buried his talent in the ground because he was afraid of what his master's response would be if he lost it. Because he squandered the opportunity to invest the talent he had been given, he was judged very harshly by his master, and his talent was taken away and given to the one who had ten.

For the purposes of this chapter, the main point I want to take away from this parable is that the master did not expect his servants to make a tenfold profit on his money. Each one was just expected to wisely invest the talents, returning a profit in proportion to what they had been originally given. Too often, Christians bury their talents in the ground instead of investing them in the kingdom of heaven. Just as an example, if God has blessed me with an ability to sing, but the only time I use it is while singing in the shower, I am essentially burying that talent in the ground. Worse yet, if I use that talent for my own glory, it would be more like spending the talent on myself than burying it in the ground.

I'll never forget the time this lesson was seared into my memory. There was an instance when I was asked to lead worship for a weekend men's retreat, and God used the opportunity to knock me down a few pegs. During the Friday night worship session I was playing guitar and singing, and I very distinctly remember thinking to myself, "Hey, the worship is sounding pretty good tonight." At exactly that moment, it became as if the words I was singing were attached to sandbags, and they began falling to the floor. I struggled through the rest of the session, and the following day I had to ask someone else to lead until I was able to gain the proper attitude of worship. On the surface, it appeared as if I was being gracious by allowing others to lead, but the reality was I just couldn't continue. The lesson was powerful: Even in Christian service, it is possible to serve yourself and your own ego under the guise of serving the King.

> *1 Corinthians 4:7 "For who makes you different from anyone else? What do you have that you did not receive? And if you did receive it, why do you boast as though you did not?"*

The Pallet of Costly Stones

Each one of us is "endowed by our Creator" with certain talents and abilities that are intended for use in the building of our wall; it is much like a pallet of costly stones dropped off at the worksite of our lives. We are given exactly what we need for the construction of our section of the wall, but the problem is that we are often more impressed by the pallet belonging to the Christian next to us than our own. Also, sometimes the stones are too weighty, so we search for wood, hay or stubble to make the construction process less draining.

Believe it or not, Moses struggled with feelings of inadequacy, and he tried to convince God that he (Moses) was a few stones shy of a full pallet. When God called on Moses to bring the Israelites out of Egypt, he responded:

Exodus 4:10–13 "O Lord, I have never been eloquent, neither in the past nor since you have spoken to your servant. I am slow of speech and tongue."

The Lord said to him, "Who gave man his mouth? Who makes him deaf or mute? Who gives him sight or makes him blind? Is it not I, the Lord? Now go; I will help you speak and will teach you what to say."

But Moses said, "O Lord, please send someone else to do it."

Can you imagine saying to God, "Sorry Bud, you're making a mistake. Pick someone else." Yet we do this every day by not responding when he calls us to use our gifts. God eventually allowed Moses to take Aaron with him to handle his public speaking engagements, but much like Moses' inability to speak, Aaron was missing his spine. While Moses was on Mount Sinai receiving the Ten Commandments, the Israelites grew impatient and convinced Aaron to let them worship a golden calf.

Flawed

I hope I didn't just shatter your image of Moses—you know the one: the white, flowing beard, the thundering voice, flames shooting out of his eyes, the immovable rock—but the story is meant to be an encouragement. God's servants are flawed, especially the ones who are human, but it doesn't seem to matter to Him. Somehow, in spite of our human weakness, He is able to take our feeble efforts, empowered by the Holy Spirit, and accomplish His eternal purposes. It is not humility, but sinfulness, when we say that our shortcomings are beyond the reach of God.

God has called you by name, and you are His; build with the precious stones he has given to you.

> *Isaiah 43:1 But now, this is what the Lord says—he who created you, O Jacob, he who formed you, O Israel: "Fear not, for I have redeemed you; I have summoned you by name; you are mine."*

Loaves and Fishes

The only one of Jesus' miracles contained in all four gospels, besides the resurrection, is the feeding of the five thousand, and in my opinion, it is the one most relevant to the concept of stewardship. Much like the story of Moses, the disciples were asked to do the impossible. There were five thousand men plus their families getting hungry and probably irritable, and Jesus says to His disciples, "You give them something to eat." Their response was in the tradition of Moses:

> *Mark 6:37 They said to him, "That would take eight months of a man's wages! Are we to go and spend that much on bread and give it to them to eat?"*

Keep in mind, Jesus knew full well what He was about to do, but He wanted His disciples to learn this valuable lesson. He told them to find out how many loaves they had available, and all four Gospels say that the disciples rounded up five loaves and two fishes. The Gospel of John gives a little more detail by explaining that it was a young boy who sacrificed his loaves and fishes for the cause.

Now, I find it hard to believe that out of several thousand people, only one child or his parents had the sense to think ahead and pack something to eat. It is more likely he was the only one generous enough to share; he was probably not old enough to realize he was supposed to be selfish and hoard it for himself. The most natural reaction would have been, "If I give it to you, then what will I have to eat?" Who knows, maybe his parents were behind him speaking with a forceful whisper through clenched teeth, "Put that food away before someone sees it! . . . Oh, hi, John and Phillip. Of course you can take the loaves and fishes; anything for the Christ." Sometimes it takes the faith and purity of a child for Christ to be able to work His miracles in our lives.

I believe the primary lesson we should learn from this miracle is that Jesus will take our meager offering and multiply it exponentially to accomplish the seemingly impossible. In real life terms, when we feel overwhelmed by the task of attempting to live a godly Christian life this secular culture, all Christ asks of us is to give the few loaves and fishes we have—to return to Him the talents and resources He has blessed us with. It is up to Him to accomplish the miracle, not us. There are times when I feel as if what I have to offer amounts to nothing more than a crouton and an anchovy, especially when it comes to parenting, but I need to offer it anyway, trusting in God's faithfulness. I suppose Jesus could have done just as well with one loaf and one fish, or even none at all, but He still wants us to offer all we have.

Our eyes should not be focused on how few loaves and fishes we have or even on the tremendous multitude Jesus intends to feed with them, but on Christ himself. Similarly, our eyes should not be focused on how much of the wall has been smashed down and needs rebuilt or on how few precious stones with which we have to build, but on Christ himself. A faithful steward takes the talents he has been given and invests them in the kingdom of God, and as a result, will one day hear the words, "Well done, good and faithful servant."

Stewardship of the Body

There are countless areas of stewardship within the context of the Christian journey, but the only other one I would like to examine more closely is the stewardship of the body. There are so many ways in which this particular area affects the other two (stewardship of finances and talents), that I believe this chapter would be incomplete without it.

The mantra of the day in regard to our bodies is this: "It's my body. I own it, and nobody has the right to tell me what I'm allowed to do in the privacy of my own home." But those who consider themselves Christians will have a difficult time supporting this stance with Scripture.

> *1 Corinthians 6:19–20 "Do you not know that your body is a temple of the Holy Spirit, who is in you, whom you have received from God? You are not your own; you were bought at a price. Therefore honor God with your body."*

The "price" referred to here is that of the cross, and when we accept Christ's sacrifice for our sins, we are essentially handing over the deeds for our bodies to His Holy Spirit. We no longer have the right to do whatever we want, and so dishonor God. It's not that we ever really owned our bodies in the first place, but it is more like an overdue acknowledgment of who really does own them.

Like a Bad Habit

Many Christians will demonize self-destructive behavior like smoking or overeating, and to be sure, God is displeased when we voluntarily destroy the work of His hands, but Christ pointed out that the issues of the heart were far more important. The Pharisees and the teachers of the law were always focused on the external appearance of impropriety, and in the book of Matthew, Jesus takes the opportunity to correct them:

> *Matthew 15:17–20 "Don't you see that whatever enters the mouth goes into the stomach and then out of the body. But the things that come out of the mouth come from the heart, and these make a man 'unclean.' For out of the heart come evil thoughts, murder, adultery, sexual immorality, theft, false testimony, slander. These are what make a man 'unclean'"*

I don't wish to minimize the noble goal of staying healthy, but it needs to be kept in perspective. It is ironic that we'll put such a high premium on keeping ourselves physically fit, but we have no qualms about polluting our minds and our hearts with sexual sin and the ungodly entertainment of our culture.

> *1 Timothy 4:7–8 . . . train yourself to be godly. For physical training is of some value, but Godliness has value for all things, holding promise for both the present life and the life to come.*

So with all of these disclaimers and qualifiers in mind, self-destructive habits and addictions *do* become overtly sinful when they begin destroying God's perfect plan for our lives. For example, if the occasional drink becomes an every day necessity, it starts to destroy our ability to be able to function as men and women of God. Our marriages will begin to struggle, our finances will be wasted, and our witness to those around us, including our children, will be rendered useless. The end result will be a complete disregard for the work of God's hands.

> *Isaiah 5:11–12, 22 Woe to those who rise early in the morning to run after their drinks, who stay up late at night till they are enflamed with wine. They have harps and lyres at their banquets, tambourines and flutes and wine, but they have no regard for the deeds of the Lord, no respect for the work of his hands . . . Woe to those who are heroes at drinking wine and champions at mixing drinks . . .*

It is not my desire to run through a long list of vices and what

Scripture has to say about them, because the pattern is similar for all of them. Suffice it to say, just about every earthly thing in life can become sinful if not done in moderation and within the confines of God's Word. The Apostle Paul's approach was to avoid being mastered by anything, even if it was not intrinsically sinful.

> *1 Corinthians 6:12–13 "Everything is permissible for me"—but not everything is beneficial. "Everything is permissible for me"—but I will not be mastered by anything. "Food for the stomach and the stomach for food"—but God will destroy them both.*

The primary consideration when dealing with these areas of potential sin is to be open to the prompting of the Holy Spirit because only Christ knows our vulnerabilities. Also, as a parent, I would rather err on the side of restraint than tempt my children to sin. I have no way of knowing what my children will one day struggle with, but I would be foolish to allow my present actions play a part in their future demise. Also, as Christians, we should be careful not to flaunt the strength we have in a particular area at the expense of those who are struggling.

> *1 Corinthians 8:9, 12–13 "Be careful, however, that the exercise of your freedom does not become a stumbling block to the weak . . .*
>
> *. . . When you sin against your brothers in this way and wound their weak conscience, you sin against Christ. Therefore, if what I eat causes my brother to fall into sin, I will never eat meat again, so that I will not cause him to fall."*

In this particular case, Paul was speaking about eating food sacrificed to idols, but the basic principle can be applied universally.

Free-Love and Peace, Man

Given the current state of sexuality in America, I would say the stewardship of our passions—or lack thereof—has done more to destroy the spiritual foundation of this country than just about anything else. But as I mentioned in chapter 8, the abandonment of God preceded this moral slide.

> *Romans 1:24 Therefore God gave them over in the sinful desires of their hearts to sexual impurity for the degrading of their bodies with one another.*

We have been told by the great thinkers of our day that unbridled sexuality is a good thing, and only the unenlightened try to restrict sexual freedom. I would like to ask the woman or child enslaved by the porn industry whether or not unbridled sexuality is a "good thing." I also wouldn't mind getting an opinion from all those suffering from sexually-transmitted diseases or from the woman whose husband can't shake his addiction to pornography. Why not also ask the opinion of the fifteen-year-old girl and her boyfriend, who are forced to make the adult decision of choosing between life and abortion for their unborn child? And while we're polling people, let's talk to the divorced couple and their devastated children about how helpful that adulterous affair was to their marriage and family. And finally, to all the women who bought into the "empowering freedom" of the sexual revolution of the sixties and seventies: Are you starting to feel as if the joke was on you? Are you starting to get clued into why so many men were saying at the time, "Hey, now that's a movement I can support"?

> *Ephesians 4:17–19 "So I tell you this, and insist on it in the Lord, that you must no longer live as the Gentiles do, in the futility of their thinking. They are darkened in their understanding and separated from the life of God because of the ignorance that is in them due to the hardening of their hearts. Having lost all sensitivity, they have given themselves over to sensuality so as to indulge in every kind of impurity, with a continual lust for more."*

As Christians, if not as human beings, we need to face the hard truth: We are far worse off as a result of this "revolution," and it is going to take something of a revolution to reverse it. The brave men and women who have fought and died to maintain the freedom we now enjoy have had their sacrifices dishonored by what we have done with this freedom. The passage I quoted earlier from the book of Romans points out that we "degrade" each other when we use each other as objects of pleasure and engage in sinful behavior. Even for those who have the best of intentions and plan to marry, sex outside of marriage is against God's will, and it is still considered fornication. We can dress it up a little and call it premarital love, but Scripture still says the "sexually immoral" will not inherit the kingdom of God.

Now it would be foolish for any of us to think we are in a position to judge the eternal condition of another's soul, but it would be equally foolish to think a person can sin willfully and without remorse and still be confident of their salvation. If someone has the ability to overlook portions of Scripture for their own benefit, it is time to start praying for that person's soul. Within that last thought lies the whole premise and motivation for this book: It is time for those of us who know the Truth to stop pretending as if we do not. I would rather offend someone close to me, than to be a party to their destruction. I'd rather endure twenty years of the "silent treatment" or even verbal daggers if it means getting to eventually see them in heaven for eternity. It is time to stop tip-toeing around each other and to start speaking the truth in love.

The Christian Mindset

> *Ephesians 5:3–8 "But among you there must not even be a hint of sexual immorality, or of any kind of impurity, or of greed, because these are improper for God's holy people. Nor should there be obscenity, foolish talk or coarse joking, which are out of place, but rather thanksgiving. For of this you can be sure: No immoral, impure or greedy person—such a man is an idolater—has any inheritance in the kingdom of Christ and of God. Let no one deceive you with empty words, for because of such*

things God's wrath comes to those who are disobedient. Therefore do not be partners with them. For once you were darkness, but now you are a light in the world. Live as children of the Light… and find out what pleases the Lord."

As we learn to be faithful stewards of this magnificent creation—the human body—a Christian mindset will begin to take shape, and the Holy Spirit will give us the strength to live and to talk and to think as "children of the Light."

Once again, the whole principle of stewardship is the realization that nothing we have belongs to us. Our money will one day be gone or given to someone else, our talents will eventually cease—either today or twenty years from now, and our physical bodies will return to the earth. So we need to enthusiastically offer our loaves and fishes and let Jesus multiply them for His glory.

Romans 14:7–8 "For none of us lives to himself alone and none of us dies to himself alone. If we live, we live to the Lord; and if we die, we die to the Lord. So, whether we live or die, we belong to the Lord."

CHAPTER 14
the legacy of the spirit

"God With Us"

"You give them something to eat."

So far, we have covered the first two dimensions of a person's legacy—the precious stones of human talents, abilities and resources put into service for God, surrounded by the mortar of relationships holding it all together. But there is a third dimension that makes this wall we are building eternally relevent, and our analogy would be quite lacking without it. In the previous chapter, I alluded to it by introducing the story of the loaves and fishes, shifting the focus away from human effort and toward Christ. When He spoke those baffling words, "You give them something to eat," He wasn't toying with them just to see their reaction; he was essentially saying, "As long as I am here with you, you have everything you need to do as I have asked."

In the Gospel of Mark, Jesus teaches his disciples a similar lesson as they are about to be capsized in a storm. Verse 4:37 says, "A furious squall came up, and waves broke over the boat, so that it was nearly swamped." In many ways, this scenario was like the feeding of the five thousand. I don't believe Jesus was taken by surprise by the sudden storm any more than he was surprised that five thousand people were hungry after a long day of teaching and healing. Oddly enough, during the storm "Jesus was in the stern, sleeping on a cushion." His act of snoozing while the disciples panicked was synonymous with His command "You give them something to eat." And the response of the disciples to the sinking of their boat was very similar to their response when asked to feed the five thousand; "Teacher, don't you care if we drown?" Again, Jesus was essentially saying, "As long as I am here with you, you have nothing to fear."

Who is this man?

The most natural response to the possibility of drowning is to panic, but this is exactly the point Jesus is trying to make; when we receive Him, we put aside the natural in favor of the supernatural. How often do we feel like saying, "Um, Jesus . . . a little help here . . . the boat is swamped and I could use a little help bailing"? As you may know, Jesus did finally calm the storm, and then He asked them, "Why are you so afraid? Do you still have no faith?" After witnessing the miracle, their response was one of terror and awe, not jubilation.

> *Mark 4:41 "They were terrified and asked each other, 'Who is this? Even the wind and the waves obey him!'"*

In spite of the miracles they had witnessed up to that point, there was a sudden realization that He was far more than a miracle worker and a great teacher; the familiarity and camaraderie they had developed suddenly vanished, and it was replaced with the fear of God. As we mature in our Christian faith, any buddy-buddy aspect of the relationship should become tempered with the awesome awareness of being in the presence of the Almighty God. It is easy to become overly familiar with Jesus, treating Him like an imaginary pen-pal and less like the God of all creation. He does seek a deep, personal relationship with us, but it should be balanced with a healthy amount of majestic fear. For the disciples, the sinking boat scenario started with a fear of their circumstances and ended with the fear of the Lord. If the Lord is to be our sanctuary when the waves begin crashing over the boat, it must start with the same fear or terror experienced by the disciples *after* Jesus calmed the storm.

> *Isaiah 8:12–14 " . . . do not fear what they fear, and do not dread it. The Lord Almighty is the One you are to regard as Holy, he is the One you are to fear, he is the One you are to dread,* **and he will be a sanctuary.**" *(emphasis added)*

This same lesson was being taught through the multiplication of the loaves and fishes: If we learn to realize that we are in the presence of God, we will not despair when He says, "You give them something to eat."

God With Us

One of the names used in Scripture pertaining to Christ is Immanuel, meaning "God with us," and it is this very realization that represents the third and most important dimension of this whole idea of building a legacy. Setting about the work of building the wall is ultimately useless if it is not inspired and carried out by the Spirit of Christ. The first thought that probably comes to mind is, "Yeah, it was easy for the disciples; they had Christ with them for real. They literally had 'God with us.'" But as I mentioned in chapter six, Christ did not leave us as orphans when His physical body returned to heaven; He gave us His Spirit. Once again, I would like to quote this promise Jesus made to us.

> *John 14:15–18 "If you love me, you will obey what I command. And I will ask the Father and he will give you another Counselor to be with you forever—The Spirit of Truth. The world cannot accept Him, because it neither sees Him nor knows Him. But you know Him, for He lives with you and will be in you. I will not leave you as orphans; I will come to you."*

The Divine Foreman

The Holy Spirit is not a sort of secondhand Jesus but the very Spirit and Presence of Christ. This *is* "God with us." As we stare at the crumbled sections of the wall, it is easy to feel orphaned, as though God created the earth and then abandoned us, watching from afar as we destroy each other. And then we hear the words "You fix it. You rebuild the wall." At this command our response needs to be, "Lord, I have three pebbles and a teaspoon full of mortar. Let's get to work." It is the responsibility of the Holy Spirit to then multiply our offering, to give us the specific tools we need to build, and to give us the daily guidance and know-how for using these tools.

In this work of building the kingdom of God—and consequently our legacy—the Holy Spirit serves as a divine foreman, and the gifts of the Spirit represent the tools. Ultimately, these tools are to be used for the purposes of building and edifying the Church; a spiritual legacy will result from this work only if our focus remains on building God's kingdom. These gifts are not given to us to be buried in a jar in the ground, but to be used for the common good of the Church.

> *1 Corinthians 12:4–7 "There are different kinds of gifts, but the same Spirit. There are different kinds of service, but the same Lord. There are different kinds of working, but the same God works all of them in all men."*
>
> *"Now to each one the manifestation of the Spirit is given for the common good."*

It is God's desire to lavish His Spirit on all who earnestly seek this blessing.

> *Luke 11:11–13 "Which of you fathers, if your son asks for a fish, will give him a snake instead? Or if he asks for an egg, will give him a scorpion? If you then, though you are evil, know how to give good gifts to your children, how much more will your Father in heaven give the Holy Spirit to those who ask him!"*

As members of God's Holy Church, I believe we tend to seriously undervalue the role of the Holy Spirit, both in our daily lives and in the work of building God's kingdom. The tendency is to want to make decisions based on common sense or practical experience, forgetting that we possess the Spirit of Christ. This approach inevitably leads to the equivalent of sending home the five thousand and missing the miracle-working power of God. When we invite the Holy Spirit to bring the power of God to our decision making process, suddenly, every aid to that process—whether it is pastoral care, human intellect, conscience or even common sense—takes on a supernatural wisdom. Very often, we find (after the fact) that many aspects of the decisions made through God's Spirit could not have been foreseen, humanly speaking—and our faith is strengthened.

The Deposit of Future Glory

In addition to the Spirit's role of daily guidance, we need to remember that Christ promised this gift to us as sort of a down-payment guaranteeing our future glory; otherwise we would spend the rest of our days vainly searching for some assurance of our salvation.

> *Ephesians 1:13–14 "Having believed, you were marked in him with a seal, the promised Holy Spirit, who is a deposit guaranteeing our inheritance until the redemption of those who are God's possession—to the praise of his glory."*

"But you will receive power . . ."

Steadfast faith in the assurance of our eternal salvation is one of the defining characteristics of a man or woman who has received this gift of the Holy Spirit. Consequently, a truly spiritual legacy is one marked by the power and the gifts of that same Spirit. This is such a crucial element to the spiritual effectiveness of the life of a Christian that Jesus himself warned the disciples (after His resurrection but before Pentecost) not to attempt to spread the Gospel before they had received the outpouring of His Spirit at Pentecost.

Acts 1:4–5, 8 "Do not leave Jerusalem, but wait for the gift my Father promised, which you have heard me speak about. For John baptized with water, but in a few days you will be baptized with the Holy Spirit . . . But you will receive power when the Holy Spirit comes on you; and you will be my witnesses in Jerusalem, and in all Judea and Samaria, and to the ends of the earth."

" . . . wait for the Gift my Father promised . . ." The most natural reaction to Christ's resurrection would have been for the disciples to excitedly run from house to house sharing the good news, but it would have been mere human effort, void of the power of God. One of the most vivid examples of trying to do spiritual work without the power of the Spirit is found in the book of Acts.

Acts 19:13–17 Some Jews who went around driving out evil spirits tried to invoke the name of the Lord Jesus over those who were demon-possessed. They would say, "In the name of Jesus, whom Paul preaches, I command you to come out." Seven sons of Sceva, a Jewish chief priest, were doing this. One day the evil spirit answered them, "Jesus I know, and I know about Paul, but who are you?" Then the man who had the evil spirit jumped on them and overpowered them all. He gave them such a beating that they ran out of the house naked and bleeding.

When this became known to the Jews and Greeks living in Ephesus, they were all seized with fear, and the name of the Lord Jesus was held in high honor.

The Flight of the Spiritual Bumblebees

The men in the passage above gave the appearance of busily serving God, but they were missing the defining characteristic of His Holy Spirit, rendering them unrecognizable to the demonic spirits and powerless to do God's will. These men, though they were not

Christians, were attempting to invoke the name of Jesus as if it were a tool of sorcery.

But as Christians, a more common way of being caught doing "spiritual" work without the Spirit is to be working outside of the will of God. When I served in the army, there were a few guys in my unit who figured out that if they looked busy, it was unlikely they would be asked to "volunteer" for any actual work. So if one of our superiors was walking toward us, the guys would quickly do something to appear hurried, like take out a set of keys and flip them in their hands while walking at a determined pace. The superior was led to assume, "Oh, he must be going to sign out a truck. I better assign this tedious task to someone else." (I have also been told that carrying a push-broom works just as well.)

Very often, as Christians, we take the same approach to service in the Church. "Uh-oh . . . here comes God. Hurry up . . . look busy!" In some cases, the busyness is an attempt to make up for the areas of our personal lives in which we fall short—in other words, a desperate attempt to balance the scales a little in preparation for Judgment Day. But in many cases, it is the natural reaction to recognizing a legitimate need and desiring to meet it. In other words, we notice the wind and the waves, and we start frantically bailing instead of asking God to calm the sea of need. The quickest path to spiritual burnout is to attempt to meet the never-ending needs of a hurting world.

Four Days Late

No one was more aware of the desperate condition of the world around Him than Christ, yet He didn't rush from place to place attempting to heal every sickness and mend every broken heart. There were even times when His seemingly cavalier attitude was part of the greater purpose of bringing glory to the Father. For example, in the case of Lazarus, He waited a couple of extra days before He responded to Mary and Martha's request to come heal their sick brother. By the time He arrived, Lazarus had been dead for four days, and only

Martha came out to meet Jesus as He arrived; Mary undoubtedly was at home dealing with some issues of resentment. In their view of the circumstances, Jesus was four days late in coming to the assistance of the people He considered friends. As we all know, Lazarus was raised from the dead, but during the prior four days of anguish, Mary and Martha were still led to believe that Jesus had broken the promise He made when He said to them, "This sickness will not end in death. No, it is for God's glory so that God's Son may be glorified through it." (John 11:4)

The point is—a life led by the Spirit of God will not be a frenzied and chaotic effort to save the world. This is not to say that there won't be times when we feel pushed to the limit, but there should be an underlying peace that keeps us anchored as the storms rage around us. It is an awareness of "God with us" in the boat. There will be times He will appear to be napping or "four days late," but this is the very time we are to rely on the promise of peace through His Spirit—God with us.

> *Isaiah 26:3–4 You will keep in perfect peace him whose mind is steadfast because he trusts in you. Trust in the Lord forever, for the Lord, the Lord, is the Rock eternal.*
>
> *Philippians 4:7 "And the peace of God, which transcends all understanding, will guard your hearts and your minds in Christ Jesus."*

Christ was able to be at peace with not healing every disease and feeding every stomach because He came to earth with a clearly defined mission and purpose, which was nothing less than the salvation of all humanity; every hour of every day was spent in support of that purpose.

Given a Trust

If Christ's primary mission was to provide the way to the heavenly Father through His death and resurrection, the mission of those of us who have chosen to accept that sacrifice is to safeguard the corresponding gift of His Spirit by devoting our lives to the service of His kingdom. This outpouring of the Spirit is entrusted to us, much like material wealth or the gift of relationships, and like those—only to a far greater degree—we must prove to be faithful stewards of this trust.

> *1 Corinthians 4:1–2 "So then, men ought to regard us as servants of Christ and as those entrusted with the secret things of God. Now it is required that those who have been given a trust must prove faithful."*

Again, this Spiritual trust is what makes it even possible to be faithful with the other two areas of the legacy. As we build with the precious stones we have been given, surrounded by the relationships entrusted to us, the Holy Spirit guides our hearts and our hands, ultimately resulting in the strengthening of our families, our churches and our nation.

Love, Obedience & Power

In chapter six, I mentioned that there is a unique relationship between the three concepts of loving God, obeying God and the outpouring of His Holy Spirit, and I would like to revisit this point as a way of bringing the three components of the legacy together. If the defining characteristic of the spiritual legacy is the working of the Holy Spirit, then it must follow that the most spiritual life is the one marked by obedience to God, since Christ makes obedience the prerequisite to witnessing the power of the Spirit.

> *John 14:15 "If you love me, you will obey what I command. And I will ask the Father and he will give you another Counselor to be with you forever—The Spirit of Truth."*

> *Acts 5:32 "We are witnesses of these things, and so is the Holy Spirit, whom God has given **to those who obey him**." (emphasis added)*

Our love for God is evidenced by our obedience to His commands, and the power of His Spirit follows. Over and over again, Scripture points to obedience as the clearest indicator of our love for God and the authenticator of our position as disciples.

John 8:31–32 To the Jews who had believed in him, Jesus said, "If you hold to my teaching, you are really my disciples. Then you will know the truth, and the truth will set you free."

If we truly love God, obedience to Him is not a burden but the key to a victorious Christian life.

1 John 5:3–5, 10, 12 "This is love for God: To obey his commands and his commands are not burdensome, for everyone born of God overcomes the world. This is the victory that has overcome the world, even our faith. Who is it that overcomes the world? Only he who believes that Jesus is the Son of God . . . Anyone who believes in the Son of God has his testimony in his heart . . . He who has the Son has life;"

Now we're getting somewhere. Our human nature tends to cringe at the mere mention of the word "obedience," but the last passage helps trim some of the sharp edges from it. Obedience is the key to life—the spiritual life and legacy—and the key to overcoming the world. In obedience to the Father, Christ allowed Himself to be crucified on the cross, and our first act of obedience as Christians is the acceptance of that sacrifice. The obedience of *One* provided redemption for all, and just as obedience opened the door to salvation, obedience to the words of God provides a foundation for a legacy that will withstand the torrents of life and the onslaught of the enemy.

Luke 6:47–48 "I will show you what he is like who comes to me and hears my words and puts them into practice. He is like a man building a house, who dug down deep and laid the foundation on rock. When a flood came, a torrent struck that house but could not shake it, because it was well built."

You'll notice it says, "When the flood came . . ." not, "If the flood comes." The torrents *will* strike, but in Christ, we will not be shaken.

Real Life Obedience

So what does this concept of obedience mean to the normal Christian who isn't floating around six inches off the ground and surrounded by a golden glow? It means that the *appearance* of spirituality is a whole lot less important than an obedient heart. For example, if I believe God has called me to coach my daughter Karine's soccer team as a means of being a Christian example to the players, but I decide to start a Bible study instead, I have neglected the more spiritual act. As another example, if someone has the gift of service or administration, but that person decides to join the choir because it looks like more fun, he or she does the whole church a disservice, and the Holy Spirit is unlikely to bless his or her efforts.

Additionally, obedience is not only pertinent to gifts and service, but to sin. It is possible to be involved in all the right activities that will best utilize my talents and spiritual gifts, but a dark little corner of sin or addiction will drain the power of the Spirit from my efforts to serve God. Just as obedience allows the Spirit to work, disobedience to God and His scriptures will hinder the power of God. It is not that the Holy Spirit is removed from a Christian because he commits a sin, but patterns of sin cause God to withdraw His favor and spiritual working from our lives. This is an important distinction, otherwise Christians would regularly flop back and forth between being saved and unsaved.

Proving Faithful

In the days of Jesus, the scribes and Pharisees put a lot of effort into making themselves appear spiritual; they would pray on the street corners and wear long, flowing robes with tassels, and when they fasted they would make sure everyone knew about it. So when Jesus began teaching that the condition of the heart was more important than outward appearance, it was a slap in the face, and they realized He was a threat to their power base. Their worst fears were realized when, after the resurrection, the disciples disregarded their position of power and decided to obey God instead.

> *Acts 4:18–20 Then they (the high priests) called them in again and commanded them not to speak or teach at all in the name of Jesus. But Peter and John replied, "Judge for yourselves whether it is right in God's sight to obey you rather than God. For we cannot help speaking about what we have seen and heard."*

"For we cannot help speaking about what we have seen and heard." This particular line jumps out at me when I think about the transforming power of the Holy Spirit, but it also reiterates the point that we have been "given a trust," and to each of us it will mean something different. There are times when the Holy Spirit entrusts a child of God with a particular spiritual gift or a passion, and when this happens, we "must prove faithful." For some, it might be a passion for evangelism or rescuing the unborn, while for others it might be an overwhelming compassion for the poor or the elderly. Still others might have the gift of healing or teaching, but for all it will mean proving faithful with what we have been given. The Apostle Paul wrote to Timothy and encouraged him not to neglect the spiritual gift he had received:

> *1 Timothy 4:13–16 "Until I come, devote yourself to the public reading of Scripture, to preaching and to teaching. Do not neglect your gift, which was given you through a prophetic message when the body of elders laid their hands on you."*

> *"Be diligent in these matters; give yourself wholly to them, so that everyone may see your progress. Watch your life and your doctrine closely."*

"Now it is required that those who have been given a trust must prove faithful." God, in His perfect wisdom, chose to pour out His Spirit differently and uniquely on each one of us, and the Church suffers greatly when any one of us buries that treasure in the ground. For me, this book represents a "trust," and I only pray that I have proven faithful. My passion is to assist as many people as possible in their journeys toward living holy and righteous lives for Jesus Christ and to play a small part in helping our nation reverse its moral slide. If you have been given such a precious treasure, don't waste it, and don't let others discourage you from proving faithful. And don't worry; God is not in the business of hiding spiritual gifts from His people. This is what Jeremiah had to say about his gift of prophecy:

Jeremiah 20:9 ". . . his word is in my heart like a fire, a fire shut up in my bones. I am weary of holding it in; indeed, I cannot."

Counting the Cost

In the passage from Acts 4:18–20, the disciples could "not help speaking about" what they had seen and heard, even though for many of them it would result in death. Inevitably, proving faithful rarely results in applause, but often in ridicule, abuse, strained relationships or, in many cases around the world, even martyrdom. The verse I quoted from Jeremiah is actually preceded by his lament that speaking God's word has brought him much ridicule and pain.

Jeremiah 20:8—9 "So the word of the Lord has brought me insult and reproach all day long. But if I say, 'I will not mention him or speak any more in his name,' his word is in my heart like a fire, a fire shut up in my bones. I am weary of holding it in; indeed, I cannot."

When put into context, the passage takes on a whole new meaning; adding the extra verse transforms it from a passionate encouragement to a stern warning: Proving faithful will come at a cost, and the faint of heart need not apply. As a matter of fact, even if you simply desire to live a godly life, there will be a price to pay for it.

2 Timothy 3:12 "In fact, everyone who wants to live a godly life in Christ Jesus will be persecuted, while evil men and impostors will go from bad to worse, deceiving and being deceived."

We need to go into this battle with our eyes wide-open but with our gaze fixed on the finish line—the opportunity to share in the future glory of Christ.

1 Peter 4:12–14 "Dear friends, do not be surprised at the painful trial you are suffering, as though something strange were happening to you. But rejoice that you participate in the sufferings of Christ, so that you may be overjoyed when his glory is revealed. If you are insulted because of the name of Christ, you are blessed, for the Spirit of glory and of God rests on you."

The Bigger Picture

I consider myself an optimist but also a realist; a large portion of this book has been devoted to showing that we live in a country that no longer celebrates the lives of men and women who are devoted to Christ. At this point in history, for most Christians I would consider the difficulties we encounter more of an inconvenience than true suffering, but as we allow our great country to continue to deteriorate, all of that could change. You can only spit in the face of God for so long before His hand of discipline comes crashing down. In this chapter, I have spent a fair amount of time on the relationship between obedience and spiritual blessing, because the same principle applies to the Church and the nation as well. The Lord speaks to His people in the same way he speaks to individuals:

Deuteronomy 5:32–33 "So be careful to do what the Lord has commanded you; do not turn aside to the right or to the left. Walk in all the way that the Lord your God has commanded you, so that you may live and prosper and prolong your days in the land that you will possess."

Isaiah 1:19–20 "If you are willing and obedient, you will eat from the best of the land; but if you resist and rebel, you will be devoured by the sword." For the mouth of the Lord has spoken.

From the beginning of time, the spiritual and material blessing of individuals, families, churches and nations has been directly linked to how seriously we take the first commandment:

Mark 12:29–30 "The most important one," answered Jesus, "is this: 'Hear, O Israel, the Lord our God, the Lord is one. Love the Lord your God with all your heart and with all your soul and with all your mind and with all your strength.'"

And if obedience is the primary indicator of our level of devotion to God, on a national level, I'd say we are seriously overdue for a correction. The correction may come in the form of God's discipline, or on the other hand, it could come in the form of a spiritual revival. But it won't be a revival unless God's people—you and I in particular—humble ourselves and repent and seek God's face.

The Spiritual Legacy

Only in a state of humility and prayer may we offer ourselves to our Creator. Then passing on a Godly legacy will be the inevitable result of surrendering our relationships, our talents, our resources, our bodies, and our spiritual gifts to the care and guidance of Christ, living a life of obedience to the voice of His Spirit. By taking personal responsibility for the section of the wall entrusted to us, the ultimate result will be a strengthening of the Church, and as the Church is strengthened, the nation will be as well. This may sound naïve and rather utopian, but we serve a God of miracles—"God with us"—and He desires to bless those who love and obey Him.

*1 Corinthians 2:9–10 "No eye has seen, no ear has heard, no mind has conceived what God has prepared **for those who love him**"— But God has revealed it to us by his Spirit. (emphasis added)*

CHAPTER 15
a time for heroes

Making it Count

Very rarely, but occasionally nonetheless, Hollywood producers will stumble across something noble in a movie script and forget to edit it out before the movie goes to production. One such example can be found in the movie "First Knight," with Sean Connery and Richard Gere. Gere plays the part of the self-absorbed-chip-on-his-shoulder-just-because-his-parents-were-murdered Lancelot, while Connery plays the noble King Arthur, and both roles were perfectly cast. At one point in the movie, King Arthur begins to recognize that Lancelot's bravery is really just a reckless disregard for his own life; Lancelot had nothing to live for, so staying alive held no significance for him. King Arthur then offers these words of advice:

"If you must die, die serving something greater than yourself."

If I could reduce the purpose of this book down to one sentence, the one above would serve the purpose as well as any. In the movie, King Arthur's advice referred to serving others by defending Camelot, which, in-and-of itself, was a noble goal. But how much nobler would it be to serve the kingdom of heaven, which unlike Camelot, will never perish?

Hebrews 12:22–24 "But you have come to Mount Zion, to the heavenly Jerusalem, the city of the living God. You have come to thousands upon thousands of angels in joyful assembly, to the church of the first born, whose names are written in heaven. You have come to God, the judge of all men, to the spirits of righteous men made perfect, to Jesus the mediator of a new covenant . . ."

"...thousands upon thousands of angels in joyful assembly..." If only we could be shown our eternal destiny once per week, or even once per year, I believe each one of us would serve God with far more fervor.

Hebrews 12:28–29 "Therefore, since we are receiving a kingdom that cannot be shaken, let us be thankful, and so worship God acceptably with reverence and awe, for our 'God is a consuming fire.'"

"If you must die . . ."

While writing this final chapter, I received a flyer in the mail designed to get me excited about the prospect of being cremated. The company boasted about their competitive rates— "Cremation now costs under $700!"—but what piqued my interest was the fact that the cremation would be done at their own "in-house" facility, so I wouldn't have to worry about my cremation being out-sourced to some foreign outfit. Once my wife and I discovered that the crematory did not offer a "Forty years, no interest, no payments!" plan, we decided we weren't quite ready to "Act now!" But we saved the flyer for holiday dinner-party conversation.

In keeping with my God-given right to employ my coping mechanism, I joke about death, but I don't particularly enjoy the topic; I don't know many people who do. But I do believe—for Christians anyway—God does not want it to be a source of anxiety. The idea of passing from this earth before knowing that each one of my children is safely and eternally in the arms of Christ has caused me significant anguish; this particular concern was one of the driving motivations for this book. But I believe if we want our lives to have eternal significance, it will start with appreciating God's perspective on death. For us, death can appear to be the worst thing that can happen to a person, but for God, it is something He views as precious; it is the means by which we are freed from the chains of sin, temptation, pain, addiction and heartache.

> *Psalm 116:15–16 Precious in the sight of the Lord is the death of his saints. O Lord, truly I am your servant; I am your servant, the son of your maidservant; you have freed me from my chains.*

This is one of my favorite scriptures because it is so contrary to normal human reasoning. For humanity, death is often viewed as an end, and for those who have freely chosen to reject Christ, it is far worse than an end. But for God's people, it is the process by which we are ushered into the "heavenly Jerusalem, the city of the Living God." I have no trouble making such a self-assured statement because I am not presently staring death in the face—as far as I know. But I only hope that when my "time" arrives, I have the grace to embrace in reality what I know to be true by faith. The level of faith each one of us has in this eternal truth is evidenced by the way we spend our lives, and more specifically, whom or what we spend our lives serving.

" . . . die serving something greater than yourself."

It is my firm belief that our Creator has placed deep within us a desire and a sense for the heroic. After all, who isn't inspired by a story about a man or woman who overcame tremendous odds and emerged victorious, or even more so, a story about someone who gave his life for another? Who doesn't imagine themselves in a similar situation being the one to rise above natural fears and inhibitions to rush into the burning building or to say, "Enough is enough!" and stand firm when no one else will? For those of us who truly believe in what Christ did on the cross—the truest example of "something greater than yourself"—our sense for the heroic should be shouting, "The time to stand is now!"

> Romans 13:11–12 *"The hour has come for you to wake up from your slumber, because our salvation is nearer now than when we first believed. The night is nearly over; the day is almost here. So let us put aside the deeds of darkness and put on the armor of light."*

"Why stand we here idle?"

I have devoted a sizable portion of this book to pointing out that our Christian faith is under attack on many different fronts. At the same time, Christians are repeatedly being asked to keep their opinions and their beliefs to themselves—and to our discredit, we submit. So I would once again like to borrow Patrick Henry's words to help inspire a response to these trends.

> *Mr. President . . . Should I keep back my opinions at such a time, through fear of giving offense, I should consider myself as guilty of treason towards my country, and of an act of disloyalty toward the Majesty of Heaven, which I revere above all earthly kings.*

Patrick Henry could speak boldly because of his deep faith and because he was not focused on the enemy but on the millions who would stand with him.

> *"Sir, we are not weak . . . The millions of people, armed in the holy cause of liberty."*

We must reach back and seize his words for our day: *We are not weak . . .* millions of Christians, *armed in the holy cause* of righteousness with the purpose of preserving the vision of our founding fathers—a God-fearing nation. We have been "endowed by our Creator," not by the government, with the unalienable right to worship our Lord openly and freely. *We are not weak . . .* we stand with Jesus Christ, our

Captain, joined by ". . . thousands upon thousands of angels in joyful assembly . . ." as we march confidently toward our eternal home.

Should we stay planted in our couches, idly entranced by uncommon "reality," as our brethren die for the faith around the world? *What is it that gentlemen wish? What would they have?* Is complacency so dear or the snares of eroticism so sweet as to be purchased at the price of addiction and slavery to sin?

> *Our brethren are already in the field! Why stand we here idle? What is it that gentlemen wish? What would they have? Is life so dear, or peace so sweet, as to be purchased at the price of chains and slavery?*

Our brethren lie bleeding in the field, enslaved, unable to reach their swords, and with each technological advancement, the dead are multiplied; the fragrance of stolen pleasures belies the stench of spiritual poverty. *Why stand we here idle?*

A Time for Heroes

> *Ecclesiastes 3:1–2 "There is a time for everything, and a season for every activity under heaven: a time to be born and a time to die, a time to plant and a time to uproot, a time to kill and a time to heal, a time to tear down and a time to build, a time to weep and a time to laugh . . ."*

Our time is a time for heroes. Our modern culture offers an endless array of comforts and distractions and pleasures—not to mention unfettered access to every type of perversion the pits of hell can offer—and all of these things are rapidly eroding what is left of this great country. The battle is intensifying, and nothing less than a heroic effort by those who lay claim to the Name and sacrifice of our Savior will suffice. But if we stand shoulder to shoulder with the saints and angels, we will die serving a cause greater than ourselves—the cause of Christ.

"...Supreme Authority and just Government of Almighty God..."

As I was contemplating the title for this book, I chose "Snowballs Taking Chances," first, because it relates to the risks individuals take with the issue of salvation. Second, because it speaks to the state of the Christian faith within "progressive" churches, as they condone and even embrace various types of sin. And last, because it defines the shaky future of a nation that devalues human life, dishonors marriage, and allows its judicial system to remove any mention of God and His Commandments from its institutions. These challenges are monumental, to say the least, but not insurmountable to a unified body of Christians willing to humbly and faithfully commit to the cause.

America and the Christian Church stand at a crossroads. At one time, the leaders of this nation felt no shame proclaiming Christ as Lord, and public policy—even official records—reflected the powerful beliefs of leaders devoted to the Christian faith. The subheading I used above is a phrase taken from an official proclamation signed by Abraham Lincoln on March 30, 1863, instituting a national day of prayer and fasting. At the time, the Civil War was devastating the country, and the proclamation was meant to drive people to their knees, desperately pleading for God's mercy. As I recently read through the document, I was stunned by the present day relevancy of it; it was as if it could have been written for our times, and it should be required reading for all Americans.

I truly believe this is a document inspired by God himself, and it was meant not only for that particular generation, but for every generation thereafter. It speaks of a nation blest beyond compare, having "grown in numbers, wealth and power, as no other nation has ever grown. But we have forgotten God." How much more relevent to our generation could it be? It held the answer for Abraham Lincoln's time, and I believe it holds the answer for ours as well. I can't possibly improve on what was written, so I would like to quote the proclamation in its entirety.

By the President of the United States of America.
A Proclamation.

Whereas, the Senate of the United States, devoutly recognizing the Supreme Authority and just Government of Almighty God, in all the affairs of men and of nations, has, by a resolution, requested the President to designate and set apart a day for National prayer and humiliation.

And whereas it is the duty of nations as well as of men, to own their dependence upon the overruling power of God, to confess their sins and transgressions, in humble sorrow, yet with assured hope that genuine repentance will lead to mercy and pardon; and to recognize the sublime truth, announced in the Holy Scriptures and proven by all history, that those nations only are blessed whose God is the Lord.

And, insomuch as we know that, by His divine law, nations like individuals are subjected to punishments and chastisements in this world, may we not justly fear that the awful calamity of civil war, which now desolates the land, may be but a punishment, inflicted upon us, for our presumptuous sins, to the needful end of our national reformation as a whole People? We have been the recipients of the choicest bounties of Heaven. We have been preserved, these many years, in peace and prosperity. We have grown in numbers, wealth and power, as no other nation has ever grown. But we have forgotten God. We have forgotten the gracious hand which preserved us in peace, and multiplied and enriched and strengthened us; and we have vainly imagined, in the deceitfulness of out hearts, that all these blessings were produced by some superior wisdom and virtue of our own. Intoxicated with unbroken success, we have become too self-sufficient to feel the necessity of redeeming and preserving grace, too proud to pray to the God that made us!

It behooves us then, to humble ourselves before the offended

Power, to confess our national sins, and to pray for clemency and forgiveness.

Now, therefore, in compliance with the request, and fully concurring in the views of the Senate, I do, by this my proclamation, designate and set apart Thursday, the 30th Day of April, 1863, as a day of national humiliation, fasting and prayer. And I do hereby request all the People to abstain, on that day, from their ordinary secular pursuits, and to unite, at their several places of public worship and their respective homes, in keeping the day holy to the Lord, and devoted to the humble discharge of the religious duties proper to that solemn occasion.

All this being done, in sincerity and truth, let us then rest humbly in the hope authorized by the Divine teachings, that the united cry of the Nation will be heard on high, and answered with blessings, no less than the pardon of our national sins, and the restoration of our now divided and suffering Country, to its former happy condition of unity and peace.

In witness whereof, I have hereunto set my hand and caused the seal of the United States to be affixed.

Done at the City of Washington, this thirtieth day of March, in the year of our Lord one thousand eight hundred and sixty-three, and of the Independence of the United States the eighty-seventh.

By the President: Abraham Lincoln

William H. Seward, Secretary of State.

Making it Count

Every heroic Christian effort begins on our knees, and as the document above calls us to a state of prayer, humility and repentance, we need to go forward with the resolve to make every aspect of our lives count for the glory of Jesus Christ, our Savior. Furthermore, our lives need to reflect the joy that comes from knowing personally the God of all creation, who goes before us to prepare an eternal home of magnificent glory.

We have been granted one earthly life to live, and we need to live it for the sole purpose of one day hearing those wonderful words, "Well done, good and faithful servant!" (Matthew 22:21)

In an effort to firmly imbed this in the minds of my children, I have a little tradition I've adopted before their bedtime prayers. Frequently I'll say to them, "You only get one chance at this life . . ." and their response is supposed to be, "Make it count!" Occasionally I'll try to trip them up and ask something like, "What's the reason you should make it count?" And they should answer, "Because you only get one chance at this life." They are just now getting to the age of being able to understand what it means to "make it count," so now, more than ever, I pray that my life represents a sacrifice worthy of the calling I have received.

Not knowing when autumn will arrive for me, or for my wife, or even for my kids, I intend to live every day for the glory of my Savior.

After all, you really *do* only get one chance at this life . . . **Make it count!**

> *Revelation 3:12 "Him who overcomes I will make a pillar in the temple of my God."—Jesus*

TATE PUBLISHING & *Enterprises*

Tate Publishing is committed to excellence in the publishing industry. Our staff of highly trained professionals, including editors, graphic designers, and marketing personnel, work together to produce the very finest books available. The company reflects the philosophy established by the founders, based on Psalms 68:11,

"THE LORD GAVE THE WORD AND GREAT WAS THE COMPANY OF THOSE WHO PUBLISHED IT."

If you would like further information, please call
1.888.361.9473
or visit our website
www.tatepublishing.com

TATE PUBLISHING & *Enterprises*, LLC
127 E. Trade Center Terrace
Mustang, Oklahoma 73064 USA